George Clooney

AN ILLUSTRATED STORY

DAVID BASSOM

HAMLYN

First and foremost, the author would like to thank Julian Brown, Karen O'Grady and all at Reed Books for their continued support, encouragement and employment. I'd also like to extend my gratitude to my 'spies' in Hollywood and Putney, and to Tessa, Mike, Danny and Bridget for keeping out of the way recently. *Now, does anyone know if there's a doctor in the house?*

Publishing Director: Laura Bamford
Executive Editor: Julian Brown
Editor: Karen O'Grady
Assistant Editor: Tarda
Design: Glen Wilkins
Executive Art Editor: Mark Stevens
Picture Research: Zoe Holtermann
Production: Julie Hadingham

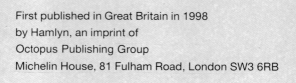

First published in Great Britain in 1998
by Hamlyn, an imprint of
Octopus Publishing Group
Michelin House, 81 Fulham Road, London SW3 6RB

ISBN 0 600 59271 5

A catalogue record for this book is available from the
British Library

Produced by Toppan
Printed and Bound in Hong Kong

Contents

Child's Play
6

Highway to Hollywood
14

Trials, Tribulations and Tomatoes
20

The End of the Road?
26

Calling Dr Ross
34

In Love and War
52

To the Batcave!
62

Out of Sight
70

Selected Credits
78

1

Child's Play

After appearing in a string of failed TV shows and lousy movies, George Clooney has finally realised the Hollywood dream

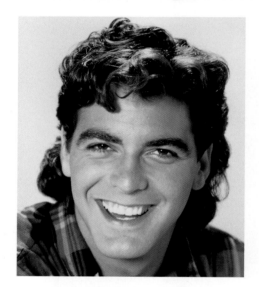

George Clooney had to wait 12 long and difficult years before he found worldwide fame and acclaim in *ER*

Above: George learned a great deal about the agony and the ecstasy of showbusiness from his father, TV presenter Nick Clooney

Opposite: A film and TV star who is popular with male and female viewers alike, George Clooney has obviously got a lot to smile about

There's just no escaping George Clooney. Switch on your TV and he'll be saving lives and breaking hearts as hunky Dr Doug Ross in America's top-rated TV series, *ER*. Visit your local cinema or video store and there'll be a wide range of Clooney's movies awaiting you, including such high-profile outings as *From Dusk Till Dawn*, *One Fine Day*, *The Peacemaker* and *Batman and Robin*. Pick up a newspaper and there's a good chance that Clooney's latest adventures, both on- and off-set, have made the headlines. And even if you just walk down the street, you're more than likely to see someone with their own variation of Clooney's trend-setting 'Julius Caesar' haircut! Honestly, there's no escaping the man.

George Clooney is undoubtedly the 1990s' hottest star: an acting sensation who made the traditionally-tricky transition from small screen hero to movie idol with enviable ease. Succeeding where a host of TV celebrities have failed, Clooney used *ER* as a spring-board to a major film career. And, even more incredibly, he achieved this feat without turning his back on the show that made him a household name. From *ER*'s first episode in September 1994, Clooney remained proud of the series and truly grateful for the effect it had upon his life and career, to the extent that he refused to 'abandon ship' when movie stardom beckoned. As the film roles mounted, the actor maintained that he would fulfil his five-year contract with *ER* and would not leave the show until the summer of 1999. Consequently, he has spent most of his 'free time' away from the *ER* set making movies and has worked numerous 100-hour weeks to juggle his film commitments with his work in the Emergency Room.

Obviously, it would seem that Clooney has the best of all possible worlds. He's a bona fide film and TV star. He's one of those rare heart-throbs who commands adoration from women without alienating his male audience. He's not only considered a major draw for viewers but is also widely liked and respected within the entertainment industry; his work on *ER* alone has won rave reviews and numerous accolades, including nominations for an Emmy and Golden Globe Award. Perhaps best of all, though, Clooney is a star who has retained his down-to-Earth good humour and common sense; realising that all good things must come to an end eventually, he refuses to listen to his own hype and is simply determined to make the most of being Hollywood's hottest star while he can.

Clooney's rise to global stardom is all the more remarkable when you consider that this is the same George Clooney who, prior to the launch of *ER*, spent 12 years as a jobbing actor and was known only to devotees of bad television and B-movies. The early part of Clooney's career comprises a string of failed TV series and lousy films, including the low-budget horror movies *Return to Horror High*, *Grizzly II – The Predator* and the now-legendary *Return of the Killer Tomatoes!* As if to make matters worse, true success frequently slipped through Clooney's fingers: he felt so uncomfortable with his supporting roles on the hit shows *The Facts of Life*, *Roseanne* and *Sisters* that he decided to leave them in their prime, and he narrowly missed-out on roles in *The Breakfast Club*, *Reservoir Dogs* and *Thelma & Louise* that would almost certainly have been his ticket to stardom.

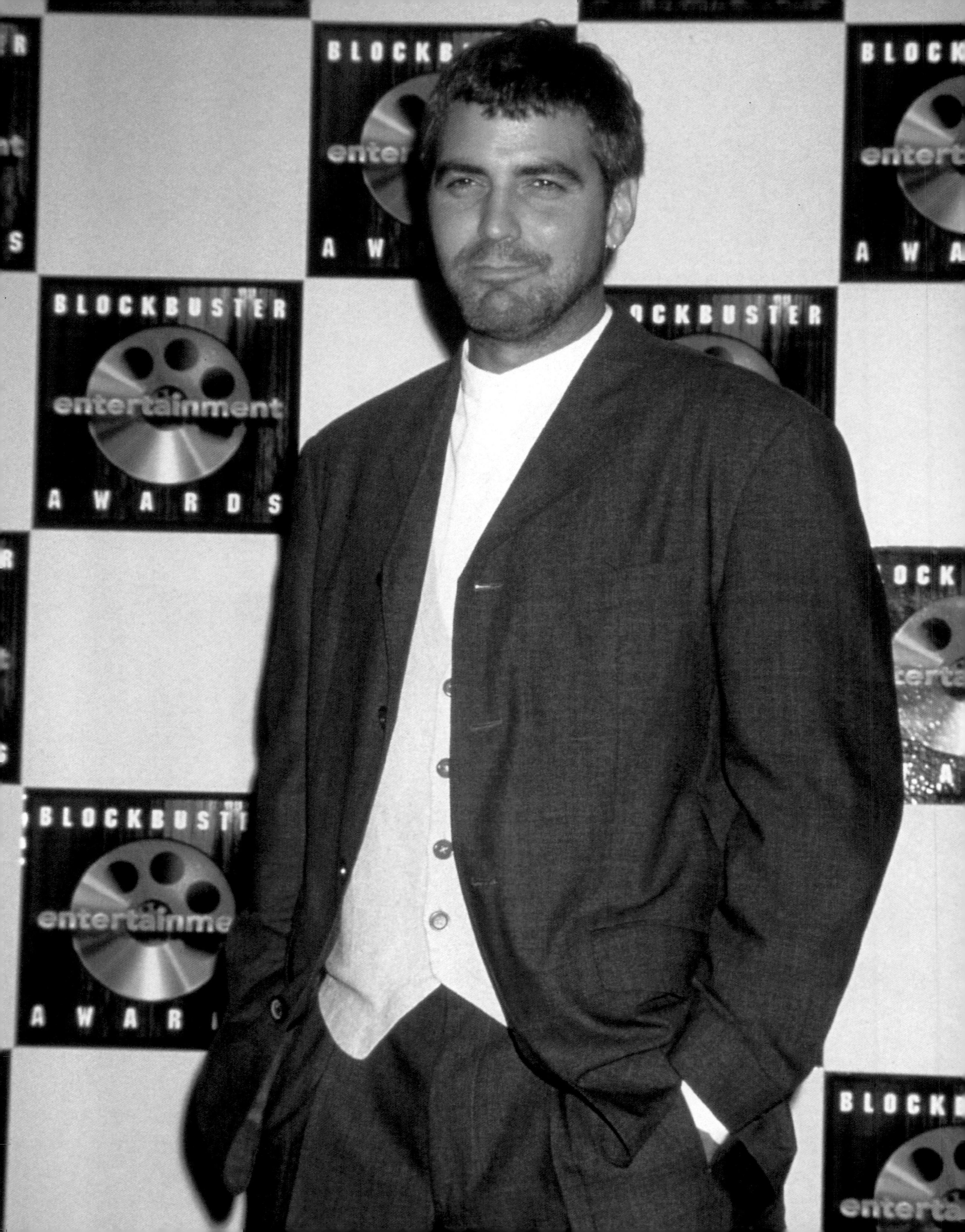
BLOCKBUSTER
entertainment
AWARDS

Yet while most actors would find it hard (if not impossible) to escape from the dangerous realm of B-movie hell and terrible TV, Clooney's easy charm, hard-working attitude and genuine sincerity somehow managed to keep his career alive, up to the critical moment when he entered the *ER*. As Clooney was propelled into the spotlight and hailed as an 'overnight success', few could deny that he had paid his dues and earned his moment in the sun. Similarly, no-one could argue with the fact that he has become one of the most popular and busiest actors working in Hollywood today.

With the benefit of hindsight, you could say that George Clooney was always destined to be a star. As a member of the Irish-American Clooney dynasty, George came from an unusually strong showbusiness background and grew up surrounded by a number of famous relatives: his father, Nick, was a highly-successful TV newscaster in America's Midwest; his great uncle George (after whom he was named) was a popular radio presenter; and his aunt, Rosemary, was one of America's best-loved singers during the 1940s and 1950s, whose acting credits included *White Christmas*. As if to strengthen the Clooney showbiz ties, Rosemary was married to the Academy Award-winning actor José Ferrer (*Cyrano de Bergerac*, *Ship of Fools*) during the 1950s and 1960s, while George's mother, Nina, was a local beauty queen who dreamed of becoming a famous dancer, until commitments to her husband and two children nipped those plans in the bud. With this brief overview of the Clooney family tree in mind, it's easy to understand why George once quipped that 'everyone in my family is famous.'

Born on May 6th, 1961 in Lexington, Kentucky, George Timothy Clooney was Nick and Nina Clooney's second child, arriving a year after his sister, Ada. Even as a baby, it seemed that George had the best of all possible worlds: on seeing him for the first time, relatives noted that he had inherited his mother's looks and his father's verve and energy!

George and Ada had a happy but decidedly unconventional upbringing. Their father, Nick, had been deeply upset by his parents' divorce when he was a child, so he

decided that his wife and children would stay with him come what may, and follow him wherever his career led. As a result, George and Ada spent much of their youth in various radio and television stations in midwest America, where they gained first-hand experience of the entertainment industry, including what it was like to be famous – Nick Clooney was a very popular local celebrity, and was frequently stopped on the streets by fans.

'My father had a variety show in Cincinatti, Ohio, among other places,' George later recalled, 'and I was always around that, either going on live TV or watching my father deal in the microcosm of a society where he was a big star. So I had some inkling of the business, and looking back I was kind of groomed for it in a way.'

Entranced by the medium, it was only a matter of time before George followed in his father's footsteps. Thus, on St Patrick's Day 1966, five-year-old George Clooney stepped in front of the camera to make his screen début – as a leprechaun! George's first appearance was so successful that he became a regular attraction on his father's show, playing such diverse roles as the Easter Bunny and a Christmas Snowman (presumably, all the costume changes were good practice for playing the Caped Crusader in *Batman and Robin*). The young actor also tried his hand at commercials, filming adverts for potato crisps and vacuum cleaners.

George, it seemed, was a natural. He simply loved acting and even joked about becoming a famous movie star when he grew up! Ada, on the other hand, decided that an actor's life was not for her and happily stayed behind the scenes.

As a child, George learned all about the painful realities of the entertainment industry. In 1968, the young actor discovered the importance of ratings when *The Nick Clooney Show* was cancelled due to a fall in its audience. George then witnessed the fickle nature of the television industry, as his famous father suddenly found himself unemployed and broke.

The transient nature of success in showbusiness was further illustrated that same year by the fortunes of George's aunt, Rosemary. Following the break-up of her

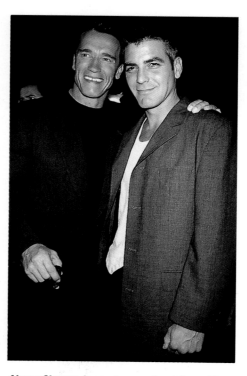

Above: Clooney is no stranger to mixing with stars like Arnold Schwarzenegger – most of George's relatives are celebrities!

Opposite: A frequent guest at award ceremonies, Clooney has received numerous accolades over the past few years

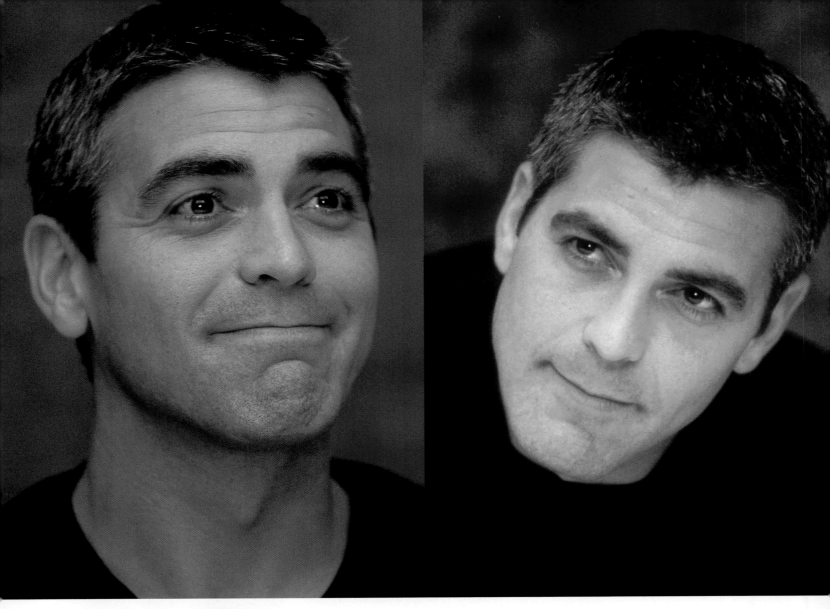

As a student at Augusta High School, Clooney was known for his wit, his gift for mimicry and his love of practical jokes …

marriage and the collapse of her career, Rosemary had become addicted to prescribed drugs and was forced to seek medical treatment. Rosemary's fall from grace had a major impact on her nephew's later life and career.

'The really important lesson came from Rosemary,' George explained, 'who was as big a singing star as you could be in 1950, but by 1960 she wasn't. Rock 'n' Roll had come in, things had changed and it had nothing to do with her talent. She didn't handle it very well, because she believed them in 1950 when they told her she was brilliant and she also believed them in 1960 when they told her she'd lost it.

'The lesson is that you're never as good as they say you are, and never as bad when they tell you you're bad.'

Fortunately, Clooney's early lessons in showbusiness weren't totally depressing, as he also observed how quickly a run of bad

luck could end. Within a few weeks of his show's cancellation, Nick Clooney found work in Mason, Ohio, followed by a stint in Bluegrass State.

Nick was subsequently offered the prestigious post of news anchor at Cincinatti's WKRW Channel 12. In a bid to provide his family with a sense of stability, he decided to move to Augusta, Kentucky, where his children would spend their teenage years.

The move didn't come a moment too soon. Prior to joining Augusta High School, George had attended no less than five primary schools. 'It was like *Gulliver's Travels*,' he claimed. 'I'd go from one school where I was the idiot to the next one where I was a genius!'

Changing school is always difficult for a child, but it is doubly-difficult for a child with a famous father. Every time Clooney enrolled in a new institution, he would soon find

himself caught-up in a battle to prove himself and win the respect of those around him. It was a battle he didn't always win.

'We'd move into a new neighbourhood and, just because of who my dad was, I'd have to get in fist-fights to prove that I wasn't a wuss,' he explained. 'And I was the worst at it. Everybody kicked my ass.'

Luckily, Clooney's experiences at Augusta High School were far better. He settled-in quickly and was very popular with his classmates, who would remember him for his wit, his ability to mimic people and his love for staging practical jokes. Surprisingly, however, he wasn't remembered as a local heart-throb; George had few girlfriends as a teenager and just didn't seem to have the time to date anyone on a regular basis.

Although Clooney continued to work on his father's shows while studying in Augusta and still joked about becoming a movie star, he had actually set his heart on pursuing a

different career – to be a professional baseball player. At the age of 16, it looked like his dream was about to come true when he was invited to try-out for his local team, the Cincinatti Reds. Unfortunately, however, he lacked a good throwing arm, and was rejected by the club.

George Clooney left Augusta High School in the summer of 1977, still devastated that his dream had been dashed. Uncertain of what he wanted to do with his life, Clooney decided to consider his future over the Summer holidays. During the break, he and his friends earned some 'easy money' by working as extras on *Centennial*, a TV mini-series which was being filmed in Augusta. Ironically, despite his experience on both this production and his father's various shows, the future film and TV star had never seriously considered becoming an actor and remained convinced that his future lay elsewhere.

… Yet while he loved entertaining his classmates, Clooney had no real desire to pursue a career in showbusiness. Instead, he wanted to be a professional baseball player!

Highway
to Hollywood

2

After appearing in his first film, Clooney was hooked. 'I fell in love with the whole industry,' he explained. 'I never thought I'd make any money at it, but I just loved doing it'

As the summer of 1977 drew to a close, George Clooney still wasn't any closer to finalising his future. In desperation, he fell back on the obvious idea of following in his father's footsteps and becoming a broadcaster. On learning of his son's plans, Nick convinced him to formally study journalism at college and agreed to fund his education. George chose to attend Northern Kentucky University, simply because many of his friends were going there.

For Clooney, university was an endless party. He had an incredible time in Kentucky, and enjoyed a full social life. Unfortunately, he did so at the expense of his studies; towards the end of his course, Clooney looked certain to fail his degree. Realising the gravity of his situation, the aspiring journalist took a part-time job at a local TV station, which he hoped would enable him to embark on a full-time career in journalism before he flunked college.

It was at this difficult moment in Clooney's life that fate dealt him an extremely lucky break – in the form of a phone call from his cousin, actor Miguel Ferrer (*RoboCop, Twin Peaks*). Ferrer called to invite Clooney to the set of a movie he was shooting with his father, José, and brother, Rafael. Entitled *And They're Off*, the film was a family drama set against a horse-racing background and was about to start filming in Lexington. Clooney agreed to meet him on location, and planned to shoot a set report which he hoped would further his career as a journalist.

Ironically, Clooney's trip to observe the filming of *And They're Off* was actually destined to end his career as a journalist. While on location, Clooney's smouldering good looks caught the eye of the film's director, who offered him a small role in the movie. Clooney decided to give it a try, and ended up spending three months in

George had a difficult time living with his aunt, singer-actress Rosemary Clooney, during the summer of 1982

Lexington, where he shared his cousin's hotel room. By the end of his vacation, Clooney had decided what he wanted to do with his life.

'I fell in love with the whole industry,' he later explained. 'I never thought I'd make any money at it, but I just loved doing it. I loved the attention. It was very seductive. There were all these beautiful women paying attention to all these guys in the movie. Then the director is saying things like, "You ought to be an actor too", and I'm thinking, "Well, yeah, maybe I should be an actor." Finally I'd found something I was really and truly interested in.'

And They're Off ultimately proved to be a non-runner, as the film was never released. Nevertheless, its place in cinematic history is now secure, as it marks the launch of George Clooney's acting career. Once shooting had finished, Clooney immediately started to plan his move to America's acting capital, Los Angeles.

While Clooney was thrilled by the prospect of acting for a living, his parents were less than impressed; in fact, his father told him he was 'crazy'. Nevertheless, George's mind was made up and he spent three months doing a variety of jobs – including cutting tobacco, selling women's shoes and working as an insurance agent – to save enough money to head for Tinseltown. Clooney finally left for LA during the summer of 1982, in his

Above: In a bizarre twist of fate, Clooney's first major TV role came in a hospital-based comedy-drama series called *E/R*!

Left: Clooney's experiences on the set of *And They're Off* convinced him to abandon journalism for a career in showbusiness

With acting roles few and far between, Clooney took a series of jobs – including working as an insurance salesman – to pay the bills

the sense that we would all be sitting around in the living room and they'd say, "Okay, let's all go to dinner. George, you stay here."'

In the meantime, Clooney's acting career was going nowhere. With a résumé consisting of a bit part in an unreleased movie and an unbilled, non-speaking role in a mini-series, he couldn't even find an agent to represent him, let alone win acting roles. Clooney attended an average of an audition a week, and faced rejection after rejection.

Clooney made a number of friends in Hollywood, though, including Tom Matthews. Consequently, when Rosemary asked her increasingly irritable nephew to leave her home, Clooney moved into Matthews's walk-in cupboard. Matthews was amazed that someone could live in his wardrobe – and even more amazed he could convince a string of girlfriends to visit him there! Among Clooney's guests at the time was actress Talia Balsam, who would later become his wife.

To pay the bills, Clooney once again took a series of jobs. Among other things, he sold insurance and men's suits, worked as a builder and, most bizarrely, was hired to draw caricatures in a mall!

As time went by, Clooney became increasingly perplexed by his failure to win acting roles. Discussing his problems with Migel Ferrer, Clooney realised that confidence was a key element in any successful audition – and it was the one thing he completely lacked. He outlined his findings to *E-TV* magazine.

'TV is weird,' he said. 'The best actor never gets the job. You get the job, or not, the minute you walk in the door because, in a way, TV is not about acting. It's about confidence.'

It was an act of supreme confidence that earned Clooney his first Hollywood gig – in a commercial for Japanese stereos. Clooney casually walked into his audition with a six-pack of chilled Japanese Sappro beer and asked if any of the casting agents wanted a drink. The actor would later credit those beers for landing him the job!

In a bid to bolster both his confidence and his acting ability, Clooney decided to enrol in an acting class. He studied under a well-respected tutor, Milton Katselas, and appeared in a number of local stage productions.

beat-up Monte Carlo car (which he worryingly christened the 'Danger Car'). At the time, he had precisely $300 to his name.

The aspiring actor spent his first few months in Hollywood staying at Rosemary Clooney's home. Sadly, living with his aunt proved to be one of the worst experiences of George's life. He earned his keep by working as Rosemary's unpaid handyman: his chores included household maintenance and chauffeuring. Quite understandably, the 22-year-old swiftly began to feel like a poor relation.

'I will never really be over the sense of how humiliated I was at that time,' Clooney subsequently told *Premiere*. 'Humiliated in

Acting class had the unexpected result of winning Clooney an agent, who spotted him during one of his first stage appearances. His agent swiftly landed him a part in his second movie: *Grizzly II – The Predator*.

A typical B-movie romp, *Grizzly II* pitted a group of young Americans against a killer bear. The film was shot on location in Budapest, Hungary, which doubled un-convincingly as northern California, and featured three actors who would go on to bigger and far better things: Platoon's Charlie Sheen, Jurassic Park's Laura Dern and, of course, George Clooney. Although the film was produced for the video market, it never actually made it to stores and was destined to become Clooney's second unreleased movie. Thus, his career was back to square one.

Or so it would have seemed. In reality, however, the film actually helped land Clooney his first starring role in a TV series. A few months after *Grizzly II* completed production, one of the movie's casting agents began working on a new half-hour comedy-drama series and immediately thought that Clooney would be an ideal choice to play one of the show's supporting characters. Clooney's audition subsequently convinced its producers that he was the man for the job.

Clooney made his début as a series regular on a TV show in September 1984. In a bizarre twist of fate, the series was called *E/R* and was set in an Emergency Room in a Chicago hospital. But it is there that the similarities with the show that made Clooney a star end.

E/R Mark I starred Elliot Gould (*M*A*S*H*, *The Long Goodbye*), Mary McDonnell (*Dances with Wolves*) and Jason Alexander (*Seinfeld*), and featured Clooney as 'My Place' Ace, a womanising hospital porter. 'I played a dimwit,' the actor joked, 'and I played him perfectly.'

Unlike its namesake, *E/R* was hardly a critical or commercial hit. An uneasy blend of comedy and drama, the show was a disaster in the ratings and was cancelled after only eight weeks.

Fortunately, *E/R*'s failure didn't reflect badly on Clooney at all. As a member of the show's supporting cast, he could not be held responsible for its lacklustre performance. So *E/R* actually represented good experience for

the rising actor: it provided him with a regular salary, generated some nice publicity and gave him invaluable experience of working on a weekly TV show.

Following *E/R*'s demise, Clooney signed a four-month contract with ABC Television. Although the contract didn't actually lead to any work for the actor, it did at least provide him with further income. Clooney then returned to the stage, appearing in *Vicious* at the prestigious Steppenwolf Theatre. The actor would always refer to this production as the pinnacle of his theatre career.

While working on the stage, Clooney auditioned for a role in a teen-orientated film drama directed by John Hughes. The movie was called *The Breakfast Club* and would go on to become a huge success at the box office. Clooney read for the role of the lead delinquent, but came second to Judd Nelson. This was the first of several occasions on which Clooney narrowly missed out on movie stardom.

Clooney consoled himself with a guest-starring role in *The Golden Girls*, and then landed a regular role in a popular drama series called *The Facts of Life*. Joining the series at the start of its sixth season, Clooney played George Burnett, a local carpenter and handyman.

From his first appearance in September 1985, Clooney's role in *The Facts of Life* was plain and simple: he was the show's heart-throb. It was a role he performed perfectly. The show's predominately female audience simply adored him as Burnett, and the fan-mail flooded in.

As the show's sixth season drew to a close, everyone was happy with the incredible hunk. Everyone, that is, apart from Clooney himself. The actor had grown tired of the 'heart-throb' label and felt that he had done everything he could with the role. Consequently, he stunned NBC and Warner Brothers by turning down an extremely lucrative deal to stay with *The Facts of Life* for another season.

Clearly, George Clooney would not allow his career to go in a direction he felt uncomfortable with. And his decision to leave *The Facts of Life* wasn't the only time that he would surprise Hollywood by not following the path he was supposed to.

Clooney's function in *The Facts of Life* was plain for all to see – he was the show's resident hunk!

Trials, Tribulations and Tomatoes

Turning his back on TV, Clooney decided to concentrate on big screen roles. But with good films few and far between, the actor soon ended up in a series of dire B-movies

Following his surprise departure from *The Facts of Life* in the spring of 1986, George Clooney decided to avoid 'beefcake' roles and focus his attention on his film career. Although working in television was both enjoyable and extremely lucrative, movie-making seemed more challenging and rewarding to Clooney. Unfortunately, the up-and-coming actor was about to learn that good roles in high quality films are few and far between.

Still hot from *The Facts of Life*, Clooney did not have to wait very long for his next project: a telemovie called *Combat High*. A madcap comedy, *Combat High* aimed to do for military training schools what the *Police Academy* movies had done for police recruitment. While Clooney showed a natural flair for comedy as Biff Woods, *Combat High* was a sub-standard affair which bombed in the ratings.

On graduating from *Combat High*, Clooney returned to the stage, where he appeared in local productions of *South Pacific*, *In My Father's House* and *Wrestlers*, the latter alongside Miguel Ferrer. He then agreed to make a cameo appearance in the low budget horror flick *Return to Horror High* as a favour to the film's writer, Greg Sims. *Return to Horror High* was a routine *Friday the 13th* clone, which featured Clooney as Oliver, a character who (wisely) disappears within the film's opening 15 minutes.

With *Return to Horror High* under his belt, Clooney was soon deluged with scripts for low-budget horror movies. In a bid to avoid typecasting, he deliberately avoided the genre, and instead took guest-starring roles in the mainstream TV shows *Hunter* and *Murder, She Wrote*.

However, when his career came to a temporary halt towards the end of 1987, Clooney decided to read one of the many horror scripts he had been sent. Much to his surprise, he found it 'hysterically funny' and immediately called the producers to express his interest. The film was called *Return of the Killer Tomatoes!* and was destined to become the most notorious project that would ever bear George Clooney's name.

A decidedly tongue-in-cheek horror adventure movie, *Return of the Killer Tomatoes!* pitched Clooney against a bunch of giant vegetables with plans to rule the

Above: Clooney's 11-stone black Vietnamese pot-bellied pig, Max, has become Hollywood's most famous pet

Opposite: Although its script was 'hysterically funny', *Return of the Killer Tomatoes!* proved to be one of Clooney's biggest embarrassments

Earth. Although the film contained a few nice moments, it was largely an embarrassment, characterised by bad jokes and lame dialogue, including Clooney's now-classic line, 'That's the bravest thing I've ever seen a vegetable do.' The actor himself was hardly impressed by the finished product, claiming that it didn't do justice to the original script. Nevertheless, the film amassed a cult following, especially in the wake of Clooney's rise to fame.

Realising that his movie career was going nowhere, Clooney decided to return to the small screen. He would establish himself on TV, and then use his success as a springboard to movie stardom. 'It's not the kiss of death,' the actor reasoned. 'Most of them, starting with Eastwood, had television series. It's just finding the right one.' Sadly, it would take Clooney many years – and even more disappointments – before he found the right show.

Clooney began auditioning for TV roles in earnest in the spring of 1988, and one of the first shows he read for was a new ABC sitcom called *Roseanne*. The series was set to become a smash hit and would make its leading actors, Roseanne Barr and John Goodman, household names. Clooney was supposed to audition for a guest-starring role in the show but, in a stroke of luck, was accidentally given the dialogue for a supporting character, Booker Brooks – a chauvinistic manager at the plastic factory where Roseanne and her sister Jackie (Laurie Metcalf) worked. Clooney's reading promptly landed him the role.

Right from the start, *Roseanne* was famed to be a difficult set to work on. Roseanne Barr had a very specific vision for the show and challenged anyone who disagreed with her.

Clooney, however, had a terrific time on the series. The easy-going actor never became embroiled in any of the on-set arguments, and got on well with the show's star. 'She was hysterical,' he later said of Miss Barr. 'She was the foulest woman I ever met – and I thought I was foul!'

The cast and crew of Roseanne widely appreciated Clooney's warm sense of humour and his penchant for practical jokes. According to co-star Sara Gilbert, he soon became the show's undisputed class clown.

'He always has something funny to say,' she told *TV Guide*. 'He'll pretend to vomit up food or dislocate his neck or do anything revolting. But he can pull it off because he is so charming all the while.'

Clooney's charm was equally appreciated by viewers. During Roseanne's first season, Booker Brooks swiftly became one of the show's most popular characters. As the fan mail poured in, Brooks's appearances became increasingly regular and John Goodman even started to joke about it suggesting the character should star in his own spin-off series!

Yet for Clooney himself, starring in *Roseanne* just didn't feel quite right. First and foremost, he wasn't at the heart of the show's success – at one point, he tellingly described himself as 'the seventh banana in the number one show.' So staying with *Roseanne* would not help him land those leading roles in movies. Clooney had also felt rather uncomfortable with his character on the show: Booker Brooks was supposed to be one of Roseanne's many enemies, but was in danger of becoming the show's resident male heart-throb.

Consequently, Clooney chose not to stay with *Roseanne* beyond its first season. Just as he had done with *The Facts of Life*, the actor turned down a lucrative offer to stay with a popular show. But Clooney felt that his future lay elsewhere.

While shooting *Roseanne*, Clooney started dating actress Kelly Preston (*Twins*, *Jerry Maguire*). The pair met at a party given by their agent, and embarked on a true whirlwind of a romance. They bought a $1 million home together a mere 23 days after their first meeting, and became engaged soon afterwards.

As two rising stars, Clooney and Preston quickly caught the attention of the press. The couple participated in a series of interviews to tell the world how happy they were, and Clooney revealed that he had bought his girlfriend a rather unusual pet: a half-blind, 11-stone black Vietnamese pot-bellied pig called Max!

Unfortunately, Clooney and Preston's romance soon went up in smoke. By the summer of 1989, Preston had moved out of their home and was engaged to Charlie

Sheen, as a prelude to her eventual marriage to John Travolta. Clooney, meanwhile, maintained 'custody' of Max.

On the rebound from Preston, Clooney turned to his former girlfriend Talia Balsam for solace. The couple soon resumed their romance and married in Las Vegas (by an Elvis look-alike, no less!) in October 1989.

The marriage seemed doomed to fail from their wedding night. After the ceremony, Clooney started to drink heavily and spent the evening at the gambling tables. Clearly, the actor wasn't quite ready for life as a married man, and he was destined to divorce Balsam three years later.

'When I became George's wife,' Balsam later told Vanity Fair, 'it was as if he didn't even like me. He spent more time with his friends than with me. He didn't seem interested in our marriage.'

Clooney agreed completely with his ex-wife's assessment of the situation, blaming himself for the failure of their relationship. 'I probably – definitely – wasn't someone who should have married at that point. I just don't feel like I gave Talia a fair shot. I was responsible for the failure of that marriage.'

The collapse of George Clooney's whirl-wind marriage was just one of several factors that would make Clooney question his career and drive the actor to the brink of despair in the early 1990s.

As Booker Brooks, Clooney swiftly became one of the most popular characters in *Roseanne*. But the actor himself felt unhappy with his role in the show, and quit at the end of its first year

***Far left:* While starring in *Roseanne*, Clooney enjoyed a brief but heavily publicised relationship with actress Kelly Preston**

Situated high in the Hollywood Hills and christened 'Casa de Clooney' by its owner, George's eight bedroom Tudor house is said to be the ultimate bachelor pad!

4

The End of the Road?

Faced with the collapse of his marriage, the death of a loved one and a potential million dollar law suit, Clooney's future looked bleak. The dream had become a nightmare

In the eyes of Hollywood producers, *Roseanne* had firmly established George Clooney as a rising star. Once news of his decision to quit the show became public, TV networks and studios began clamouring for Clooney's services, offering him projects that would make him a household name. The first TV show he signed for was *Sunset Beat*.

On paper, *Sunset Beat* must have seemed like a Godsend to Clooney. The series was writer/producer Patrick Hasburgh's follow-up to *21 Jump Street*, the critically-acclaimed and hugely successful cop show which had launched the career of Johnny Depp. *Sunset Beat* was also being backed by American's leading network, ABC, and was assured a prime-time slot. The show's future looked nothing but bright.

Sadly, however, the sun would quickly set on this '*Beat*. Whereas *21 Jump Street* was an innovative blend of teen angst and police drama, *Sunset Beat*'s improbable mix of cop drama and rock 'n' roll had viewers reaching for the off-switch. Clooney toplined the series as Chic Chesbro, an undercover motorcycle cop who took on various psychos and drug dealers while posing as a member of a rock band! *Sunset Beat* premiered on ABC in April 1990 and was cancelled within weeks.

Clooney's first post-*Roseanne* movie fared little better. Entitled *Red Surf*, the film starred Clooney as Remar, an ex-surfing champion-turned-drugs dealer who decides to abandon his life of crime for the sake of his pregnant girlfriend (played by DeDee Pfeiffer, Michelle's younger sister). Helmed by H. Gordon Boos (the acclaimed first assistant director behind *Platoon* and *The Godfather, Part 3*), *Red Surf* promised to be a polished action-drama, but was undermined by a cliché-ridden script and ultimately went straight to video.

Although Clooney would refer to the film as one of his many disappointments, it did nevertheless mark his first leading role in a movie and won him some excellent reviews. For instance, the leading American trade newspaper *Variety* praised his performance and concluded that Clooney and Pfeiffer were *Red Surf*'s two saving graces. The couple must have had a chemistry both on and off the screen, as the pair became an item following the break-up of Clooney's marriage.

Despite the lacklustre performance of *Sunset Beat* and *Red Surf*, Clooney remained a hot property and was signed to star in another ABC TV show, *Baby Talk*. A spin-off from the *Look Who's Talking* movies, *Baby Talk* followed the life of an upwardly mobile single mom and her relationship with a working-class admirer. Connie Selleca (*Hotel*) replaced Kirstie Alley as the female lead, while George Clooney stepped into the John Travolta role.

Baby Talk should have been one of the hits of the fall 1990 TV season. Its big-screen predecessors had been immensely popular, and their premise suited the sitcom format perfectly. Yet the series became another of George Clooney's flops, due largely to its inane and repetitive scripts.

If *Baby Talk* was hard to watch, it was twice as hard to work on. The show was simply plagued with problems, and was said to be one of the unhappiest productions in

Opposite: **A group of undercover cops posing as a rock band? It can only be George Clooney's first starring vehicle, *Sunset Beat***

Hollywood. Clooney had an awful time on the series, and was even said to have been jealous of Connie Selleca when she was replaced by Julia Duffey after the show's opening episode! The actor attributed much of the ill-feeling on set to executive producer Ed Weinberger, a Hollywood veteran with a reputation for being difficult.

'There were a lot of problems on the set,' the actor later remarked. 'We had several infamous fights.'

Clooney and Weinberger's ongoing struggle came to a head one day for reasons they still dispute: Clooney claims that he objected to the producer's treatment of an actress, whereas Weinberger cites a line of dialogue as the cause of their disagreement. In any case, their argument ended with Clooney leaving the show, never to return.

Walking out of *Baby Talk* could well have meant the end of George Clooney's career. He faced a multi-million dollar lawsuit for breach of contract, while Ed Weinberger publicly condemned the actor, suggesting that he should not be hired again. In the end, though, Clooney was simply released from his contract and replaced by sitcom veteran Scott Baio (*Happy Days*, *Charles in Charge*) in *Baby Talk*'s revamped second season. The show's ratings fell dramatically in season two, proving that most viewers were only tuning in for George Clooney.

Unfortunately, popularity alone isn't enough to keep an acting career going. Few producers will hire an actor who has walked-out of his last show and been branded 'difficult' by its producer. Clooney may have been lucky to escape legal action, but he wasn't out of the woods yet.

The *Baby Talk* debacle was made even more painful by the success of *Thelma & Louise* at the box office. Just before he joined the cast of *Baby Talk*, Clooney had met *Thelma & Louise*'s director, Ridley Scott, and narrowly missed out on the role that propelled Brad Pitt to instant movie stardom. Thus, as Clooney faced the end of his career, he saw Pitt become one of filmdom's hottest properties.

Ironically, it was Ed Weinberger's barrage of criticism that might have saved Clooney from oblivion. Just four days after leaving *Baby Talk*, the actor was hired to star in a new

TV pilot, *Knights of the Kitchen Table*. When he asked producer Gary David Goldberg why he was hiring him, Goldberg apparently told the actor that he did it to annoy Weinberger!

Knights of the Kitchen Table became an unsold TV pilot, and was never picked-up for a series. On wrapping the production, Clooney agreed to meet an aspiring video shop owner-turned-writer/director called Quentin Tarantino. Tarantino, a film buff with a fondness for B-movies, knew Clooney from his work on *Return to Horror High* and *Return of the Killer Tomatoes!*, and asked him to audition for a role in a low budget crime thriller with the bizarre title of *Reservoir Dogs*.

Reservoir Dogs transformed Tarantino into the hottest writer/director of the 1990s and helped consolidate the careers of many its castmembers, including Michael Madsen, Tim Roth and Steve Buscemi. Had Clooney been a part of the film, he would have fulfilled his dream of becoming a movie star.

But once again, it was not meant to be for Clooney. Still shaken by his experiences on *Baby Talk*, his heart wasn't really in the reading for *Reservoir Dogs*. 'I did a horrible, horrible audition,' he subsequently admitted. 'I remember walking out and saying to myself, "Well, I blew that!"'

Things just went from bad to worse for Clooney. As his career teetered on the edge of an abyss, the time had come for him to begin divorce proceedings with Talia Balsam. The actor gallantly accepted the blame for their marriage's failure and hoped they could reach an amicable divorce settlement. His wife's lawyers saw things differently, however – and the divorce cost him $80,000 in fees alone!

As a result of his divorce, Clooney became Hollywood's most confirmed bachelor. 'I'll never be married and I'll never have kids,' he repeatedly stated afterwards.

Besides his divorce, Clooney also had to face up to the death of his beloved uncle, George. George died from lung cancer at the age of 64; he was unmarried, had no children and his final words were, 'What a waste.' Following Uncle George's death, Clooney vowed to live life to the max and rescue his career from the brink.

'I just decided life was too short,' he explained. 'I decided that if I walked outside and got hit by a bus then at least everybody

Another of Clooney's failed TV shows, the cop drama series *Bodies of Evidence* lasted a mere eight weeks

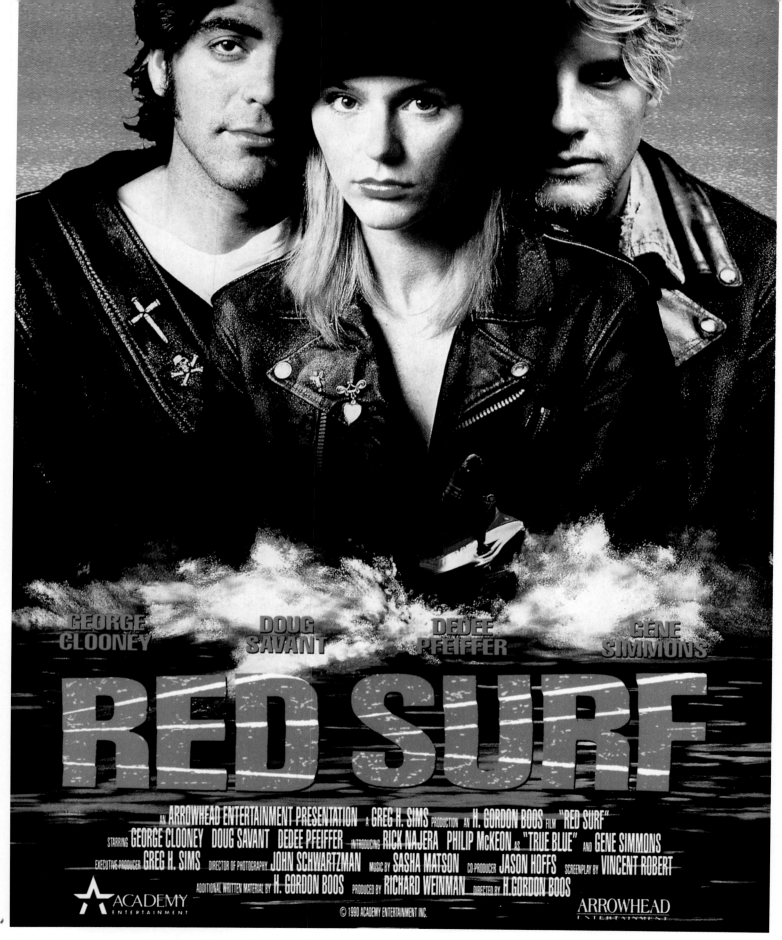

GEORGE
CLOONEY   DOUG
SAVANT   DEDEE
PFEIFFER   GENE
SIMMONS

RED SURF

AN ARROWHEAD ENTERTAINMENT PRESENTATION • A GREG H. SIMS PRODUCTION AN H. GORDON BOOS FILM "RED SURF"
STARRING GEORGE CLOONEY DOUG SAVANT DEDEE PFEIFFER INTRODUCING RICK NAJERA PHILIP McKEON AS "TRUE BLUE" AND GENE SIMMONS
EXECUTIVE PRODUCER GREG H. SIMS DIRECTOR OF PHOTOGRAPHY JOHN SCHWARTZMAN MUSIC BY SASHA MATSON CO-PRODUCER JASON HOFFS SCREENPLAY BY VINCENT ROBERT
ADDITIONAL WRITTEN MATERIAL BY H. GORDON BOOS PRODUCED BY RICHARD WEINMAN DIRECTED BY H. GORDON BOOS

ACADEMY
ENTERTAINMENT

© 1990 ACADEMY ENTERTAINMENT INC.

ARROWHEAD
ENTERTAINMENT

A routine action-drama movie, *Red Surf* did nevertheless win Clooney some good notices and
demonstrated his leading man potential

can say that, "He crammed a shitload into 34 years."'

As part of his new attitude, Clooney's already busy workload shifted up a gear. After a string of rejections, he eventually landed a co-starring role in the CBS cop show *Bodies of Evidence*. A routine affair at best, the series premiered in June, 1992 and ran for just eight weeks.

The actor then played a supporting role in *Unbecoming Age*, a fantasy-drama about a 40-year-old housewife who finds a new lease of life when she develops the ability to blow 'magic bubbles'! *Unbecoming Age* proved that Clooney hadn't lost his unique knack for appearing in truly awful films and was given a mercifully-brief release.

Clooney's career reached something of an all-time low with his next film, *The Harvest*. An offbeat thriller starring Miguel Ferrer, *The Harvest* features the future superstar in a cameo role as a 'lip-synching transvestite', who can be seen in a gay disco wearing a gold bra and dancing to the Belinda Carlisle track *Heaven is a Place on Earth*! Clooney played the role as a favour to Ferrer and had no idea the film would return to haunt him.

'It was fun and a joke at the time,' he told the *Sunday Mirror*. 'I never thought anyone would ever see it.'

The NBC telemovie *Without Warning: Terror in the Towers* provided Clooney with a much more conventional role as Kevin Shea, one of the many heroes of the disaster piece. Clooney then guest-starred in the CBS sitcom *The Building*, playing Bonnie Hunt's love interest of the week.

As he moved from one lacklustre project to another, Clooney never had any delusions about his career. He was keeping himself busy and making a great living (Miguel Ferrer tellingly referred to him as 'the richest guy in showbusiness that nobody knew'). But at the back of his mind, Clooney was still looking for a worthwhile and rewarding project to show the world what he could really do.

At this point, Clooney was offered supporting roles in two TV series. One was a brand new show, *Café Americain*, and the other was *Sisters*, a modestly successful comedy-drama series which was about to enter its third season. Clooney decided to go with the latter. It turned out be an inspired choice: *Sisters* went from strength to strength, while *Café Americain* lasted a mere eight weeks.

Like *The Facts of Life*, *Sisters* was a very much female-orientated show and featured a predominantly female cast led by Swoosie Kurtz and Sela Ward. As Detective Nick Falconer, Clooney was introduced as a love interest for Ward's character, and once again found himself as a show's resident heart-throb.

Sisters was very good experience for George. The show won high ratings and good reviews, and had the full support of the NBC network and Warner Brothers. It was also a very happy set. Clooney had no complaints; alongside *Roseanne*, he felt that *Sisters* was the best production he had been involved with.

However, by the end of his first year with the show, Clooney had once again become tired of just playing a love interest role and asked to be written out. 'It's a chick show,' he explained. 'As a guy you become all of these horrible parts, women's parts, that women have complained about for years and have every right to complain about.'

Leaving *Sisters* at the end of its third season, George Clooney was once again on the look-out for the show and the role that would make his career. Little did he know that they would be a short walk away, on the other side of the Warner Brothers studio lot.

Opposite: As Detective Nick Falconer, Clooney served as Sela Ward's love interest during the third season of *Sisters*

Below: Through good times and bad, George has remained close to his father, Nick Clooney

Calling Dr Ross

The brainchild of best-selling author Michael Crichton, *ER* launched Clooney's career into the stratosphere. After demanding an audition, he was the first person to be cast in the series

On completing his work on *Sisters*, George Clooney found himself in a very familiar position: he was once again just one TV show away from stardom. Warner Bros., who had produced *Sisters* and still had the actor under contract following his departure from the show, certainly believed that Clooney was on the verge of greatness, and offered him the leading role in *Golden Gate*, a new cop show for NBC.

Although Warner chiefs were confident that *Golden Gate* would be ideal for Clooney, the actor had other ideas. He had seen the script for the pilot episode of a new medical drama series called *ER*, and had decided that this would be his ticket to the big time.

Like many popular TV shows, *ER* had a difficult journey to the small screen. The brainchild of best-selling novelist Michael Crichton (whose numerous credits include *Jurassic Park* and *Disclosure*, to name but a few), *ER* began life way back in 1974 as a movie script entitled *EW: Emergency Ward*, and was largely based upon Crichton's own experiences as a medical student at Massachusetts General Hospital.

The screenplay languished in development hell until the late 1980s, when movie mogul Steven Spielberg expressed an interesting in directing the film. While the project was in pre-production at Spielberg's Amblin Entertainment studio, one of Spielberg's staff, Tony Thomopolous, came up with the brilliant idea of developing Crichton's original concept into a weekly series. Spielberg happily agreed and the newly-retitled *ER* was born.

However, even with Spielberg's backing, *ER* remained a risky project. American TV was dominated by half-hour comedies like *Seinfeld* and *Roseanne*; the most popular hour-long drama series, *NYPD Blue*, ranked a lowly 19th in the ratings. *ER* was also a very ambitious show, promising a big ensemble of characters and complicated, multi-plot storylines. Most unusual of all, it wasn't a conventional medical drama; unlike such shows as *Dr Kildare* and *St Elsewhere*, *ER*'s focus wasn't on the patients, but on the medical staff of Chicago's Cook County Hospital.

ER was eventually sold to the NBC network, while Warner Bros. were to supervise international distribution of the series. NBC was still playing cautious, though; whereas it had happily commissioned a full 22-episode season of Spielberg's *SeaQuest* the previous year, it initially only ordered a feature-length pilot episode of *ER* to test its feasibility.

George Clooney first heard about *ER* while it was being pitched to NBC, and he managed to get a copy of the pilot episode's script from his friend, casting director Jonathan Levey. He immediately loved the idea for the series and wanted to be a part of it. Consequently, two days after the show's pilot was commissioned, Clooney phoned executive producer John Wells to demand an audition.

'I fought to get *ER*,' the actor explained. 'I didn't think that *ER* was necessarily going to

Above: Although George Clooney was destined to be immortalised as *ER*'s Dr Doug Ross, he originally read for the role of Dr Greene!

Opposite: The *ER* episode, *Hell and High Water*, proved to be one of Clooney's very finest hours on the award-winning series

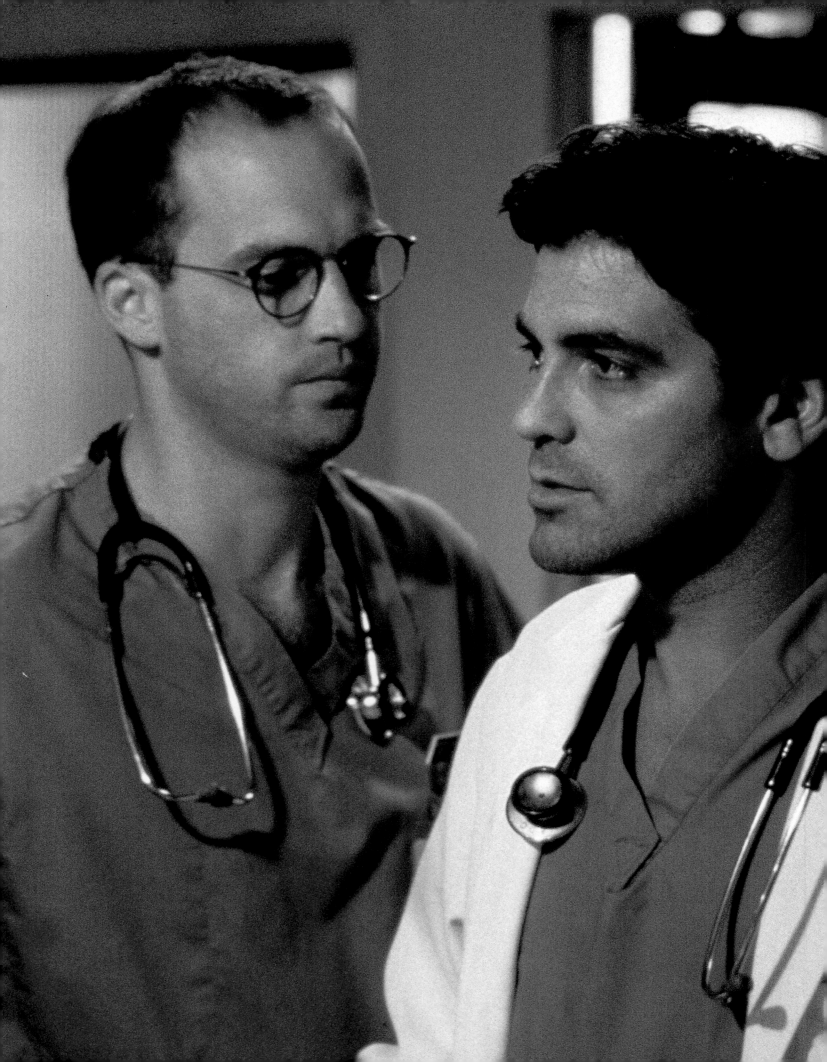

ER 's original leading cast (clockwise, from top centre): John Carter (Noah Wyle), Dr Susan Lewis (Sherry Stringfield), Dr Doug Ross (George Clooney), Dr Mark Greene (Anthony Edwards) and Dr Peter Benton (Eriq la Salle)

get picked up [as a series], because you never know. Some of the best pilots I've ever done didn't get picked up ... but I wanted to do ER. I wanted to do it because it was Spielberg, because it was Michael Crichton. It was a two hour movie of the week and, at least if it didn't go, then I had worked with Spielberg and Crichton.'

Despite his enthusiasm for the project, Clooney almost missed out on the role that made his career. The actor originally took a shine to the character of Mark Greene, the caring doctor around whom the pilot script was based, and had little interest in playing Doug Ross, who was a peripheral character in the screenplay.

Fortunately for Clooney, Jonathan Levey and ER's producers immediately sensed that he would be better cast as Dr Ross: an

immensely talented physician who is an alcoholic and womaniser outside of the Emergency Room.

'George Clooney and the Doug Ross character seemed like a complete fit,' Levey explained in Behind the Scenes at ER. 'If you're going to cast a character with behaviour you don't approve of – such as drinking too much and cheating on his girlfriend – you need someone who balances that behaviour with their innate charm and attractiveness. George is one of those people who can get away with pretty much anything because he's adorable.'

Clooney was the first person cast in ER. Warner chiefs were very happy for him to join the Spielberg-backed project and put Golden Gate back in to development Clooney considered himself to be a lucky man indeed.

Opposite: Considered a risky project by TV producers, ER was an instant smash hit, winning great reviews and even greater ratings

'That's a coup for an actor coming from the place I was coming from, which was *Return of the Killer Tomatoes!*,' he laughed. 'Up to this point, you have to remember, my career had not really been known for doing great television.'

Following Clooney's signing, the rest of *ER*'s regular cast was finalised. Anthony Edwards (*Top Gun*, *The Client*) was head-hunted for the role of Dr Mark Greene, a sensitive foil to Dr Ross, while Sherry Stringfield (*NYPD Blue*) landed the part of caring Dr Susan Lewis. Eriq La Salle (*LA Law*) made a strong impact as the no-nonsense Dr Peter Benton, Noah Wyle (*A Few Good Men*) brought a boyish charm to medical student John Carter, and Julianna Marguilies (*Homicide*, *Law and Order*) rounded up the cast as Nurse Carol Hathaway.

The pilot episode of *ER* was shot in the Spring of 1994, under the working title of *24 Hours*. The storyline followed Dr Mark Greene through a gruelling 18 hour shift and ended on a bleak note, with Nurse Hathaway being admitted to the Emergency Room after taking a drug overdose.

As soon as *24 hours* was completed, it was screened to NBC's focus groups. The network's initial fears proved ill-founded, as the pilot won a record approval rating. NBC immediately agreed to commission a full 24-episode season of *ER* and scheduled the show in the prestigious time slot: Thursday nights at 10pm.

On hearing the good news, Clooney felt confident that he was finally onto a winner. 'The minute we got picked up for Thursday night at ten o'clock I called all my friends,' he revealed. 'That's because I know television – I grew up in television – and I called all my friends and said, "My career just got made." I knew the minute we got Thursday night at 10pm on NBC.'

The pilot episode of *ER* premiered on Monday September 19th, 1994, with the weekly series claiming its regular slot the following Thursday. The show was an instant critical and commercial smash hit. Critics hailed *ER* as cutting-edge television, while viewers were simply hooked.

Within weeks of *ER*'s debut, the show's castmembers had become household names. And Doug Ross swiftly became the series'

most popular character. Clooney attributed much of Dr Ross' popularity to his flaws, and sensed that viewers sympathised with many of his dilemmas.

'Doug Ross is a guy in his mid-thirties,' he explained in *Behind the Scenes at ER*, 'who has just discovered that all the things he used to do in life – partying a little too hard and chasing the girls a little too much – are all starting to catch up with him. It's not working like it used to. He is faced with having to deal with his inadequacies as an adult.'

Clooney's terrific performance as the hard-drinking, womanising doctor made many viewers wonder if Doug Ross was just an extension of himself. But Clooney shrugged off such suggestions. 'We both live hard,' he conceded in *E-TV*, 'but he's a sad figure and I've had a great life.

'I'm also not as short as you might think either,' the 5' 10" actor added with a grin. 'All of the guys on the show are 6' 2" and

As the series developed, *ER* fans became captivated by Dr Ross's relationship with Nurse Hathaway (Julianna Marguilies)

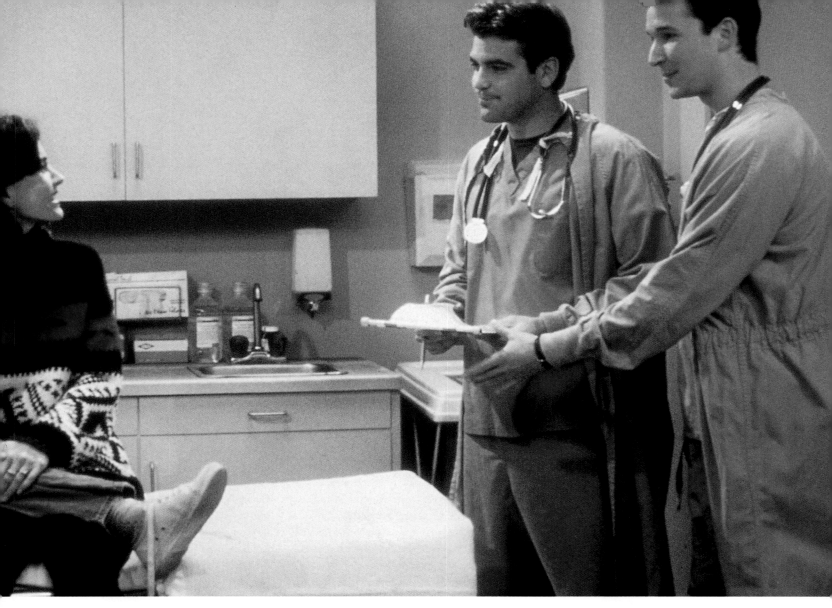

everyone seems to think that I'm a midget!'

Whereas many actors would let such instant fame and acclaim go to their heads, Clooney's feet remained firmly on the ground and he was extremely modest about his growing popularity and fame. 'It's the show,' he proclaimed. 'If you were a mannequin on that show, they'd love the mannequin.'

Nevertheless, NBC was keen to capitalise on Clooney's growing popularity and asked him to represent *ER* on some of America's top-rated chat shows, including *The Tonight Show*. At the network's behest, the actor also hosted an instalment of the long-running comedy series *Saturday Night Live* in February 1995. Clooney was more than happy to oblige his employer.

'When all this crazy stuff started to happen I was ready,' he explained. 'I've worked a very long time to get to this position.'

NBC also arranged Clooney's guest-appearance in an episode of its hot new sitcom, *Friends*. In *The One with Two Parts, Part Two*, Clooney and his *ER* co-star Noah Wyle play two physicians, Dr Mitchell and Dr Rosen respectively, who begin dating Monica (Courtney Cox) and Rachel (Jennifer Anniston) after the latter sprains her ankle. The *Friends*/*ER* crossover represented a bid by NBC to consolidate both shows' early success in the ratings, and gave Clooney and Wyle a welcome chance to offer a comic spin on their *ER* alter egos.

As the fan mail began to arrive in its millions, it became clear that Clooney was perceived as *ER*'s resident heart-throb and had more than his fair share of adoring female fans. Although the actor had publicly resisted the heart-throb tag earlier in his career, especially when he starred in *The Facts of Life* and *Sisters*, he was unconcerned by the description while starring on *ER*. Working on the show was challenging and rewarding, and Doug Ross wasn't just a love interest character.

Clooney and co-star Noah Wyle spoofed their *ER* alter egos in the *Friends* episode, *The One with Two Parts, Part Two*!

Clooney was also flattered to learn that Dr Ross had generated a substantial gay following and was amused to be labelled a 'gay icon'. He was especially touched by one piece of fan mail from a gay admirer, which he actually decided to put on display at his home.

'I have it framed and hanging in my upstairs hallway,' the actor told *E-TV*. 'It reads, "Dear George Clooney. You are my favourite star. I love you. I love homosexual men. On your movies, I'd like to see you do …"' and it goes on to specify all manner of explicit sexual acts. The note ends: "Please send me an autographed picture of you in a white shirt and tie."'

'I love that,' Clooney laughed. 'You can't make up stuff like that. Even in Hollywood.'

The actor later spoofed his status as gay icon in 1997, when he voiced Sparky in an episode of the adult animated series *South Park* entitled *Big Gay Al's Big Gay Boat Ride*!

Of course, George Clooney has never seriously been accused of being gay. Since the launch of *ER*, the tabloid press has happily portrayed him as a modern-day Casanova, and detailed his relationships with the likes of Talia Balsam, DeDee Pfeiffer, Denise Crosby (Bing's granddaughter and a semi-regular on *Star Trek: The Next Generation*), Kimberley Russell (*Head of the Class*), MTV presenter Karen Duffy and Cameron Diaz (*The Mask, A Life Less Ordinary*). Once those stories had dried up, the tabloids proceeded to link Clooney with virtually every woman he spoke to, including *Knot's Landing* star Nicolette Sheridan, supermodels Cindy Crawford and Elle Macpherson, *Friends* sensation Courtney Cox and pop superstar Madonna (whose advances the actor actually spurned at the 1995 MTV Music Awards). Most bizarrely, Clooney was even reported to be dating the Duchess of York, Sarah Ferguson, after he joked on a chat show that she wanted to sleep with him!

Fortunately, Clooney could see the funny side of the press' claims. 'If I was going out with one tenth of the girls I get accused of, I wouldn't have time to do anything,' he pointed out in *Premiere*.

Aside from Clooney's purported love life, the tabloids were also intrigued by his home: a two-story, eight bedroom Tudor house in the

Hollywood Hills, which he christened 'Casa de Clooney'. The actor shared the building with two friends, Matt Adler and Tom Matthews, both of whom had moved in following the break-up of their marriages. 'It's a *Free Willy* situation,' Clooney joked in *Movie Idols*. 'Get them back on their feet, then put them back in the ocean.' The tabloids proceeded to depict Casa de Clooney as the ultimate bachelor pad.

Meanwhile, back on the set of *ER*, the show's producers made sure that their hot new star had plenty to do. Whereas the show's pilot episode focused on Dr Greene, Dr Ross was given a much larger role in the first season. In-between medical dramas, the character embarked on a doomed affair with a single mom, Diane Leeds (Lisa Zane), and was shown to have more than a professional interest in his colleague, Nurse Hathaway.

On a more personal note, *ER*'s first season also brought Clooney's first on-screen collaboration with his aunt, Rosemary. The pair had long settled there differences since George's arrival in Hollywood in 1982, and he was delighted when she was joined the show on a recurring basis as Mary Kavanugh, a grandmother suffering from Alzheimers Disease.

ER also reunited Clooney with writer/director Quentin Tarantino, whom he had met three years previously during his legendary audition for *Reservoir Dogs*. Since their last meeting, Tarantino had become Hollywood's hottest film-maker, and was invited to helm an episode of *ER* after he revealed that he was a fan of the series.

Clooney was not only *ER*'s nominal star, but was also its resident prankster. He quickly became famed for his practical jokes and was said to be particularly lethal with his remote-controlled whoopee cushion! While the cast and crew occasionally found Clooney's behaviour distracting, more often than not they just loved it.

'There are times when you want to say, "George calm down a bit,"' Julianna Marguilies explained. 'But every now and then, to look over and see him wearing a urine container on his head just makes you feel a little bit better about your work!'

As news of Clooney's pranks became common knowledge, some members of the

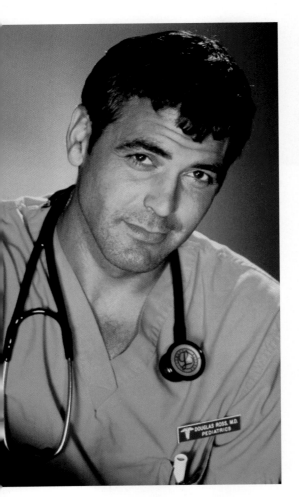

As Doug Ross emerged as *ER*'s most popular character, George Clooney swiftly became a household name

show's cast and crew tried to beat him at his own game. Unfortunately for them, however, Clooney almost always had the last laugh. Take for example, this tale of Clooney's struggle with one of *ER*'s guest directors, whom the actor wisely refuses to name.

'I was standing with a plate of spaghetti in my hands,' he recalled in *Film Review*, 'and the show's director goes, "Does that smell funny to you?" and I leaned over and he smacked the plate into my nose. He was laughing hysterically, but no one else was laughing – the cast and crew were horrified. I looked at him and said, "Are you out of your mind? I live for this!" He said, "Come on, get me!" Every day he'd say, "You got that prank?"'

'The day he was leaving, as he was getting into his $80,000 Mercedes, he said, "I guess you didn't get me, George." I had everybody come out to say goodbye to him. On the back of his car, around his license plate, I got a sign that said, "So many men, so little time!" He rode for about three and a half months before he found it!'

Clooney's pranks weren't restricted to the set of *ER*, though. In fact, his prime targets were his closest friends. Indeed, one pal fell foul of an elaborate hoax which took no less than 16 months to perpetrate! Driving around Los Angeles one day, Clooney noticed a painting of a Mexican lady that was lying in a rubbish pile. Realising that it was 'the ugliest painting' he had ever seen, the actor took it home and came up with the idea for a prank: whenever one of his golfing partners would ask the actor if he wanted to join them for a round, Clooney would say that he was too busy with his art classes and make up details of what he was learning.

Finally, after 16 months of 'art classes', Clooney visited his friend on his birthday and gave him the painting, which he had signed in its bottom right-hand corner. When Clooney said that it was his first painting and that he was proud of it, his friend had no choice but to hide his disgust and hang it up over his living room couch! The painting stayed there for three years or so, until the actor finally confessed to the gag in an issue of *Premiere*.

ER ended its first season as America's top-rated drama series, generating audiences of around 30 million viewers. The show's first

year also received a shower awards and accolades, including a staggering 23 Emmy nominations, oneof which was for George Clooney in the 'Best Actor' category. *ER* subsequently won eight Emmys, but lost out in the 'Best Series' category.

In any case, George Clooney had finally found what he has been looking for: a great role in a first-class TV series, which he could use as a springboard into movies. Now all he needed to do was make the traditionally-difficult transition from small screen sensation to big screen superstar.

Since *ER*'s launch, the tabloid press happily portrayed Clooney as a modern-day Casanova, linking him with a string of beauties

Calling Dr Ross

As the production of *ER's* first season drew to a close, George Clooney was still looking for a suitable film project to fill his hiatus. He was all too aware that the move from the small screen to the big can be perilous: while the likes of Bruce Willis and Johnny Depp used *Moonlighting* and *21 Jump Street* as stepping stones to movie stardom, most TV sensations failed to continue their success in films, and the list of recent casualties included *NYPD Blue's* David Caruso, *Northern Exposure's* Rob Morrow and *Booker's* Richard Greico. Consequently, Clooney knew that his first post-*ER* film outing would have to be chosen carefully.

'You don't want to come out and say, "Okay, now give me a million bucks and let me carry a film" the first time out after a hit television series,' Clooney explained to *GQ* magazine. 'Because then you're Richard Greico, and it's gone pretty quickly. The secret to surviving is not to go for the whole ring at once. You want to come out and do a good third or fourth lead, like Mickey Rourke in *Body Heat*.'

With strong supporting roles in good movies nowhere to be seen, Clooney resigned himself to taking the summer off, and planned to join his *ER* co-stars on an European publicity tour. But as luck would have it, Quentin Tarantino and Robert Rodriguez had other ideas for him.

Tarantino first met Rodriguez in 1992 at the Toronto Film Festival, where both directors were being hailed as rising stars: Tarantino was basking in the success of *Reservoir Dogs*, while Rodriguez was being hailed as 'one to watch' on the strength of his $7,000 action movie, *El Mariachi*. The pair immediately became friends and collaborated on the anthology movie *Four Rooms* before turning their attention to *From Dusk Till Dawn*, Tarantino's very first film script which he had written back in 1990.

Best described as *Pulp Fiction* meets *Night of the Living Dead*, *From Dusk Till Dawn* follows the adventures of Seth and Richie Gecko, two bank-robbing brothers who flee to Mexico after a bloody Texas crime spree. Whilst en route to Mexico, the Gecko boys take preacher Jacob Fuller and his two teenage kids, Kate and Scott, hostage. Once across the border, however, the group make

In a complete change of pace from *ER*, the film *From Dusk Till Dawn* starred Clooney as a mean and dangerous criminal

the mistake of stopping at The Titty Twister, a dubious bar whose clientele include a group of vampires! As soon as the sun sets, the Geckos become embroiled in a bloody battle to stay alive 'til the break of dawn.

Tarantino invited Rodriguez to direct *From Dusk Till Dawn*, and left him in charge of the film's casting. Rodriguez immediately returned the favour by asking the writer-director to play the younger Gecko brother, Richie, and subsequently cast veteran actor Harvey Keitel (*Taxi Driver*, *The Piano*) and rising starlet Juliette Lewis (*Cape Fear*, *Natural Born Killers*) as Jacob and Kate Fuller respectively. The last major role to be finalisedwas of Seth Gecko. Tarantino had conceived the character as a Humphrey Bogart-type figure and envisaged 61-year-old actor Robert Blake (of the 1970s' TV show *Baretta*) in the role. But Rodriguez wasn't convinced and soon hit upon the idea of casting George Clooney in the part.

'I was looking for someone new and fresh for the role,' Rodriguez told *Movie Idols*. 'I saw George in some episodes of *ER* and then a while later on a talk show [*Politically Incorrect*]. He was on vacation from his TV show and no-one was offering him movie roles, so we offered him the lead in our film.'

Having worked with Clooney on *ER*, Tarantino knew he was both a talented and charming individual, so he had no objection to Rodriguez's suggestion. Clooney promptly met with them to discuss the role and happily agreed to make *From Dusk Till Dawn* his follow-up to *ER*.

'What I wanted to do was a couple of good scenes in a good film,' the actor said of his decision to star in the film. 'That's what I was looking for. I did read for a couple of parts, and was offered a couple of roles, and then there were parts that I wanted to do which just weren't around. But then this came around and they said, "Do you want it?", and I said

Clooney spent a lot of time hanging out with Quentin Tarantino, so that they could develop a camaraderie that befitted the Gecko brothers in *From Dusk Till Dawn*

yes. These guys can't make bad films. That's the great thing about Robert and Quentin, they are just so talented.'

Once news of Clooney's casting became public, reporters immediately began to speculate that the actor would leave *ER* to pursue a full-time movie career. But Clooney was quick to dismiss such speculation from the outset, making it clear that he loved working on *ER*, felt proud of the show and hoped to balance his movie work with his commitment to the series.

'I have a five-year contract with the show and I'll honour it,' he stated. 'It's the right thing to do, not to mention it's really a great show and it's a great show to work on. It's hard as hell doing that show, but man I love it! I love going to work every day. I love Anthony Edwards. I love Noah Wyle. I love those people.'

Before Clooney could begin work on *From Dusk Till Dawn*, he had to reach an agreement with *ER*'s producers over his schedule. The shooting of the film overlapped with the start of *ER*'s second season, which meant that Warners would have to allow him some time off. Although the studio had no obligation to do so, executive producer John Wells made sure that the opening episodes of the season didn't feature Clooney too heavily, so that the

actor could complete his work on the movie.

From Dusk Till Dawn was shot in Mexico during the summer of 1995, according to a tight 40-day schedule. This meant that the cast and crew often had to work weekends to keep on track. The film was budgeted at $12 million, which was sparse by Hollywood standards, especially as *From Dusk Till Dawn* was packed with special effects and monster make-ups. The production was particularly hard on Clooney, who had to commute between Mexico and Los Angeles towards the end of shooting.

'I worked four days a week on *ER* and three on the film,' he told *E-TV*. 'I had to learn my lines while making the two-hour round trip between sets … I worked seven days a week for 40 days, finishing at three in the morning sometimes for *Dusk* and making it to a 6am call for *ER*.'

To play Seth Gecko, Clooney decided to change his look and adopted a new hairstyle – the short 'Julius Caesar' crop, which soon sparked a fashion trend. Clooney also spent a lot of time with Tarantino so that they could develop a camaraderie that befitted brothers. The pair visited a number of clubs and bars, and also attended the 1995 MTV Music Awards together. 'Quentin and I actually became close,' Clooney noted.

Even outside the ER, Clooney still knows how to apply that healing touch!

'It was a funny thing. We both have this kinetic energy and there is a kind of 'manicness' to both of us.'

In spite of its low budget and hectic filming schedule, a good time was had by all on the set of *From Dusk Till Dawn*. Clooney, in particular, relished the chance to break his association with Dr Ross, thus minimalising any risk of being typecast. 'It's a relief just to stick a gun in some guy's mouth and blow the back of his head off,' the actor quipped in *Cinefantastique*.

However, having spent the past year in the ER, it wasn't always easy for Clooney to abandon Doug Ross' passion for curing t he sick and saving the dying. 'In one scene, Quentin Tarantino had this really bloody hand and I started looking concerned,' the actor revealed in *E-TV* magazine. 'All of a sudden the director, Robert Rodriguez, began yelling,

"You're getting into doctor mode! Cut it out!" Then I remembered, "Oh yeah, today I'm a killer."'

During the making of *From Dusk Till Dawn*, the news broke that Clooney had been nominated for an Emmy Award for his work on *ER*. He was teased mercilessly by the film's cast and crew, and reached his trailer one morning to find a note on its door reading: 'Dear George, Emmy Schmemmy. Signed, the cast of *From Dusk Till Dawn*.'

Clooney, of course, gave as good as he got. Surprisingly, his main target was Harvey Keitel, an intense actor with a reputation for taking his work extremely seriously. Clooney would watch his co-star filming and then joke that Keitel showed promise; at one point, he even suggested that Keitel should take up acting professionally and offered to find him an agent if he moved to Los Angeles! Much to

Opposite: Clooney's legendary 'Julius Caesar' crop helped spark a fashion craze

Below: Thanks to *ER* and *From Dusk Till Dawn*, Clooney's autograph was becoming heavily in demand – even amongst his co-stars!

everyone's surprise, Keitel loved Clooney's clowning, and joined in the fun by seeking his advice and his autograph!

Another of Clooney's prime targets was director Robert Rodriguez. In an interview with *Cinefantastque*, Clooney claimed that the hot-shot director was constantly seeking his help! 'Robert is always asking me, "George how should I shoot this?" And I just tell him, "If there is some way you can just cut to me then I think you've got a movie."'

Following the completion of principal photography on *From Dusk Till Dawn*, Clooney returned to Los Angeles to concentrate his attention on *ER*. In the weeks leading up to the film's January 1996 release, Hollywood insiders began to speculate as to whether or not Clooney could attract cinemagoers. Traditional studio thinking usually dictates that moviegoers won't visit their local picture palace to see an actor who they can watch free of charge in the comfort of their own homes. Robert Rodriguez had thought of this problem, though, and promised that *From Dusk Till Dawn* would showcase a side of Clooney people would never see on *ER*.

'It's not like putting Don Johnson in an action movie where you go, "I can see that on TV for free,"' the director explained in *Empire*. 'This is an exciting actor in an exciting role playing something completely different: a complete scumbag!'

Clooney himself made it clear that *From Dusk Till Dawn* and Seth Gecko were about as far away from *ER* and Doug Ross as possible. And he was fully aware that the movie would not appeal to all of Dr Ross' admirers.

'Somebody asked me, "Don't you worry about people who watch *ER* going to see that movie?"' Clooney told *More* magazine. 'But I just said, "Anybody who goes to see a Quentin Tarantino movie knows what they're getting into."'

From Dusk Till Dawn premiered to healthy box office returns but predictably mixed reviews. An uneasy hybrid of crime thriller and B-movie gore fest, the film was super-stylishly helmed by Rodriguez but was a hit 'n' miss affair at best. In fact, the movie's strongest element was Clooney, whose portrayal of Seth Gecko was a revelation and proved that he could fill the big screen as mesmerisingly as the TV screen.

Clooney won universal praise for his work in *From Dusk Till Dawn* and went on to collect a MTV Movie Award for 'Best Breakthrough Performance.' The actor summed up the film's impact on his career perfectly in *More* magazine: 'That movie did me a lot of good, even though a lot of people didn't like it.'

Despite its shortcomings, *From Dusk Till Dawn* went on to earn cult status and spawned two made-for-video sequels (minus Clooney and Tarantino). In the wake of the film's success, Miramax released *Full Tilt*

Boogie, a documentary which follows not only the production of *From Dusk Till Dawn* but also its cast and crew's extra-curriculum activities. The documentary shows Clooney to be an extremely approachable and down-to-Earth actor, and he is frequently seen sharing a joke with the film's crew. *Full Tilt Boogie* also suggests that he lives up to his 'lady-killer' image, as he can been seen flirting with a number of his female colleagues!

As *From Dusk Till Dawn* shocked the world, Clooney was hard at work on the second season of *ER*. After making brief appearances in the season's opening episodes, Dr Ross featured in a powerful, multi-episode story arc in which a series of disputes with hospital management force him to consider a change of career.

The story arc reaches a turning point in the episode *Hell and High Water*, which sees the good doctor risking his life to save a boy from a flooding drain. The boy's rescue convinces Ross not to abandon his medical career and also proved to be one of Clooney's finest hours on *ER*; *Hell and High Water* is a brilliant showcase for the actor and one of the finest dramas *ER* has ever delivered.

The latter half of *ER*'s second season reunited Dr Ross with his long-lost father, Ray (James Farentino), thus providing Clooney with another chance to shine.

ER ended its second season not only as America's top-rated drama series but also as its most-watched TV programme overall, as it overtook the half-hour comedy *Seinfeld* to claim the top slot. Once again, the series also collected numerous awards, most notably an Emmy for 'Best Series'. Clooney, meanwhile, was nominated for several prestigious accolades, including his second Emmy Award and his first Golden Globe Award.

It soon became clear that all those hours in the Emergency Room were beginning to rub off on Clooney. While visiting Chicago, the actor joined Anthony Edwards and his family for lunch. When Edwards's three-year-old son, Bailey, began choking on a potato crisp, Clooney grabbed the child and dislodged the crisp with a firm thump on the child's back. Not content with being TV's hottest actor and a rising movie star, George Clooney was also showing promise for a career in medicine! Doug Ross would have been proud.

Above: Clooney's work in *From Dusk Till Dawn* earned him a MTV Movie Award for 'Best Breakthrough Performance'

Left: A celebrated car enthusiast, Clooney gives his *ER* co-star, Noah Wyle, a lift to work!

In Love and War

6

One Fine Day cost Clooney a small fortune, due to an agreement he had with its two child stars. 'Every time I swore I had to give them a dollar,' he explained. 'Now I think I'm paying their way through college!'

During the filming of *From Dusk Till Dawn*, Robert Rodriguez often joked that his main goal was to make George Clooney a movie star. Rodriguez's previous film, *El Mariachi*, had launched the career of Antonio Banderas (*Evita*, *Desperado*), so he simply had to give Clooney the same treatment. Consequently, while editing *Dusk Till Dawn*, Rodriguez compiled a trailer showcasing the actor and wrote some fake reviews, which he then sent to several Hollywood agents in a bid to generate some interest in the *ER* star's movie career.

'It kinda worked,' Clooney told *E-TV*. 'Studios who wouldn't throw me a bone with a small role before were now calling with big offers.'

Thanks to Rodriguez, the offers were rolling in before *From Dusk Till Dawn* had even been edited. The first studio to hire Clooney was Universal, who awarded him the leading role in its superhero action-adventure movie, *The Green Hornet*.

An adaptation of the 1930s' comic strip and the 1960s' TV series, *The Green Hornet* was set to star Clooney as Bruitt Reid, a media mogul who dons a mask to fight crime as the Green Hornet, while Jason Scott Lee (*Dragon*, *The Jungle Book*) agreed to play Kato, Reid's chauffeur and sidekick. Clooney was offered $3 million (three times his fee for *From Dusk Till Dawn*) to star in the movie and arranged to shoot it in his second season hiatus from *ER*.

Clooney's schedule became much more complicated shortly after, when the actor was offered another $3 million to play Michelle Pfeiffer's love interest in Fox's romantic comedy *One Fine Day*. Although the role had previously been turned down by movie megastars Tom Cruise and Kevin Costner, Clooney jumped at the offer.

'I knew for me, personally, that it was going to be great because I got to work with this good director [Michael Chapman] and work opposite Michelle,' he explained. 'It was such a great opportunity for me.'

Pfeiffer, whose production company Via Rosa was behind *One Fine Day*, had the final say on who was cast opposite her and asked Clooney to discuss the project with her. He was hired on the strength of their meeting.

'I had always liked George's work,' Pfeiffer later revealed. 'I hadn't seen everything, the most recent thing I had seen was *ER*, so I wasn't sure about the comedy element. But when we read through a couple of scenes together I saw he had really good comedic timing.'

Unfortunately, Clooney's commitments to *ER* and *The Green Hornet* suggested that he would not be free when *One Fine Day* began shooting in March 1996. However, Warner Brothers agreed to change his filming schedule to ensure that he could complete both projects in the hiatus before starting work on *ER*'s third season.

One Fine Day stars Clooney as Jack Taylor, an arrogant newspaper columnist who is desperately trying to balance his career with

One Fine Day demonstrated Clooney's worth as a romantic lead, in a role originally turned down by Tom Cruise and Kevin Costner

the needs of his five-year-old daughter, Maggie (Mae Whitman). While looking after Maggie, Taylor meets and falls in love with Melanie Parker (Pfeiffer), a single mother who is similarly struggling to look after her son, Sammy (*Home Alone 3*'s Alex Linz).

From the outset, *One Fine Day* was devised as an old-fashioned romantic comedy. 'I kept saying *Adam's Rib* – Tracy and Hepburn,' Clooney explained. 'We all sat down, and everybody had different ideas, but they were all from the old-fashioned comedies: make the banter quick; everything has to move; give it an old feel.'

Before filming, the actor was a little apprehensive at the prospect of starring opposite Michelle Pfeiffer. 'I was intimidated, to say the least, by working with her, because – forget she's a movie star and she's beautiful – she's one of my favourite actors. I was worried about holding up my end of my role, and she's really good that way. She'll give you an opportunity to stay in scenes with her.

That's how good she is and how competent she is. I was lucky to get that opportunity.'

Perhaps Clooney's discomfort was partly due to the fact that Michelle was the elder

Clooney's obvious rapport with *One Fine Day*'s child actors convinced Michelle Pfeiffer that he would have children of his own one day. 'Once he gets started, he'll have 10,' she claimed

Previous page: Clooney did much of his own stunt-driving in *The Peacemaker* – with explosive results!

An intelligent, story-driven thriller, *The Peacemaker* pits Lt Colonel Thomas Devoe (Clooney) and Dr Julia Kelley (Nicole Kidman) against a dangerous group of nuclear terrorists

sister of his old flame, DeDee Pfeiffer. Whereas many people would pay a small fortune to share a smooch with Michelle, Clooney apparently felt uncomfortable shooting love scenes with her and was glad to get them over with!

Besides the challenge of romancing Michelle Pfeiffer, Clooney also had to work opposite two child actors in *One Fine Day*. Much to his relief, he had an excellent time with both Mae Whitman and Alex Lintz. Unfortunately, however, the children cost Clooney a small fortune during the making of the film, due to an ill-advised agreement he made with them. 'Every time I swore, I had to give them a dollar – and if God was in there too, it was two dollars,' he explained. 'Now I think I'm paying their way through college.'

Clooney's skilled handing of his child co-stars inevitably raised the question of whether he had changed his mind about starting a family. The actor maintained that he had no such intentions.

'Kids are the ultimate responsibility,' he said when interviewed on set of *One Fine Day*. 'I think unless it's something that you absolutely have burning in you to do, you shouldn't just do it in a half-assed kind of way.

I don't really feel like messing up someone's life, you know?'

Pfeiffer, however, wasn't convinced by Clooney's rhetoric. 'He has a real love-hate relationship with children,' she noted. 'But once he gets started, he'll have 10!' Putting her money where her mouth was, she had a $10,000 bet with Clooney that he would become a father one day!

One Fine Day was shot at 44 locations in and around Manhattan, between March and May 1996. The film wrapped on May 17th and premiered on December 2nd, 1996. As an old-fashioned romantic comedy, it is One Fine Film. Clooney and Pfeiffer make a highly winning couple (despite the fact that Clooney is four years younger than his leading lady), while the kids' cute antics seldom become nauseating. The movie was well received by the critics, and performed solidly at the box office. Or so it seemed.

'*One Fine Day* was a disappointment, box office-wise,' Clooney later clarified in *Film Review*. 'I think Fox set their standards a little high for a romantic comedy. It made $100 million worldwide. That's one I make no apologies for – we did everything we set out to do with that movie.'

Following *One Fine Day*, Clooney was scheduled to start work on *The Green Hornet* for Universal. However, as the film neared production, Steven Spielberg was in the process of finalising plans for *The Peacemaker*, the first movie to be produced by his fledgling entertainment empire, DreamWorks SKG. DreamWorks had achieved modest success with its TV shows *Spin City*, *High Incident* and *Champs*, but Spielberg knew that the studio's first blig movie would have to be a serious hit to establish DreamWorks as a force to be reckoned with.

With Hollywood's finest at his disposal, Spielberg hand-picked George Clooney to play the leading role in *The Peacemaker*. And he used his personal clout to secure Clooney's services: Spielberg wrote to Universal asking the studio to release the actor from *The Green Hornet*. The powers-that-be at Universal duly obliged.

'Steven sent me a note that said, "This is our first project at DreamWorks and you're my first choice to do it,"' Clooney told *E-TV*.'

He got me out of my commitment for *The Green Hornet* so I'd be free to do it.'

Inspired by an article in *Vanity Fair* detailing nuclear weapons smuggling in the former Soviet Union, *The Peacemaker* follows the search for a group of Russian terrorists who have hijacked a consignment of nuclear warheads. As American Army intelligence officer Lieutenant Colonel Thomas Devoe, Clooney teams up with nuclear scientist Dr Julia Kelley (*Far and Away*'s Nicole Kidman) in a bid to save the post-Cold War world from annihilation.

Modestly budgeted at $50 million, *The Peacemaker* was conceived as an intelligent, story-driven thriller in the mould of *Day of the Jackal* and *Patriot Games*, as opposed to a *Rambo* or *Con Air*-style actioner. Clooney loved the premise for the film and particularly liked the idea of playing a ruthless action hero.

'This was a script that I adored,' he explained in *Film Review*. 'It was a smart suspense thriller. The film gave me the opportunity to take on a challenging and exciting role. Tom Devoe is a military expert who likes to do things his own way. He enjoys living on the edge and he does nothing by the book. But, working in tandem with the bureaucratic Dr Kelly forces him to adapt to an entirely different mode of operation in order to get the job done.'

The actor was delighted to learn that the film would be directed by Mimi Leder, a two-time Emmy Award winner for her work on *ER*. 'Mimi is the kind of director that I've always adored and that's the kind who doesn't try and make you do what they want,' he told *Empire*. 'If you don't get it right, she points you in the other direction, but she lets you do your thing first.'

Clooney started work on *The Peacemaker* on May 21st, 1996, a mere four days after leaving the set of *One Fine Day*. The film was shot in a number of locations across Europe, mainly in the war-torn remnants of former Yugoslavia.

To shoot *The Peacemaker*'s requisite car chases, Clooney took a course in stunt-driving and spent three weeks cruising around eastern Europe in a cheap Slovakian car! As soon as he got the thumbs-up from his teachers, Clooney then filmed the scene in which Devoe crashes a $130,000 Mercedes into a villain's BMW, thus halting his escape. Clooney loved stunt driving and was delighted to shoot the sequence. Much to his surprise, Nicole Kidman, had just as much fun as his passenger!

'Nicole was put in the seat,' Clooney recalled in *Film Review*. 'So I hit the BMW and thumped it into the building. She looks over at me and I say, "Are you okay?" She goes, "Harder. Hit it harder!" I said, "Okay." So we knocked it into the building a couple more times.'

Clooney evidently hit it off with his co-star and spent much of his spare time with Kidman and her husband, Hollywood megastar Tom Cruise. Cruise became one of Clooney's basketball buddies, and frequently joined him to shoot some hoops, while Kidman followed in Michelle Pfeiffer's footsteps by having a $10,000 bet with Clooney that he would become a father one day.

Having Cruise and Kidman with him during the filming provided Clooney with virtual anonymity in Slovakia, where the locals had neverseen or even heard of *ER*. 'They thought I was Tom and Nicole's bodyguard,' Clooney revealed in *Empire* magazine. 'They would come up and go, "Is it okay to go and

While filming in eastern Europe, Clooney spent a lot of his free time with Kidman and her husband, Tom Cruise – and was frequently mistaken for their bodyguard!

ask for a autograph?" It was good, I charged them $3 dollars a time.'

During a break in the production of The Peacemaker, Clooney joined Cruise and Kidman on a trip to London, to attend the British premiere of Mission: Impossible. Although he was in the country for less than 48 hours, Clooney once again managed to hit the headlines, this time being romantically linked to TV presenter Dani Behr!

The Peacemaker wrapped at the end of July 1996, and premiered in September the following year. Ultimately, it proved to be a major disappointment for DreamWorks, grossing a mere $41.2 million in the States. Although Clooney won good notices for his edgy performance as Devoe, most critics noted that The Peacemaker was let down by a plot that just seemed too familiar for its own good.

The Peacemaker may not have done much for Clooney's film career, but it did have a strong impact on his personal life. While shooting the film, the actor became involved with Céline Balitran, a 23-year-old French law student he met in Paris, where she was working as a waitress at the Barfly Café. After chatting to her for a few weeks, the actor asked Céline to join him for a Parisian stroll. 'We went for a walk and suddenly he seized me in his arms and kissed me,' she recalled in Vanity Fair. 'At that precise moment, I realised that he was the man of my life.'

Clooney felt equally strongly about the new love of his life, and invited her to live with him in Los Angeles. Céline happily moved into Casa de Clooney.

Within days of her arrival in Los Angeles, the tabloids were full of reports claiming that Céline was about to marry Clooney. However, the actor was quick to deny all such suggestions and rumours. 'The wedding? We'll hold off on that, thanks!' he laughed. 'The pig has to die first, you know – and they live for 30 years.'

The continuing popularity of ER coupled with Clooney's film career and his blossoming love life all served to intensify the media spotlight on the actor. While Clooney had always understood his responsibilities as a public figure and was happy to co-operate with the press, but a series of events in 1995

and 1996 began to make him feel that the media was overstepping the mark.

In particular, Clooney objected to the video paparazzi: amateur video camera users who would film celebrities going about their daily lives and then sell the footage to American TV shows like Hard Copy. Towards the end of 1995 and in the early part of 1996, Clooney featured in the show on virtually a weekly basis. And, quite understandably, he'd had enough.

'These kids with video cameras are not journalists. I'll be with my girlfriend and they'll say, "Who's the fat chick?" They want me to walk over to them so they can have a confrontation and sell the footage.'

In February 1996, Clooney contacted Hard Copy's producer, Frank Kelly, and struck a deal: he would continue to co-operate with its sister show, Entertainment Weekly, provided he was spared the Hard Copy treatment. The détente lasted for six months, until Kelly bought and broadcast amateur footage of Clooney and Céline. Clooney immediately responded by writing a letter to the producers of Entertainment Tonight in which he vehemently condemned the use of amateur video footage and explained why he would not co-operate with the show again.

'This thing has got to stop,' he declared. 'It seems like there are no limits on what these shows can put on air about your private life. I refuse to be stalked by video cameras every time I walk on the street … A line has to be drawn.'

Clooney's stand against the video paparazzi struck a nerve across Hollywood – once the details of his letter became public knowledge, a number of celebrities, including Madonna, Steven Spielberg and Whoopi Goldberg, all offered to join his campaign against the practice. Faced with such widespread condemnation for there actions, Paramount Pictures (the production company behind Entertainment Tonight and Hard Copy) swiftly announced that it would no longer buy or broadcast amateur footage.

Clearly, George Clooney had scored a major victory for what he believed in. With the furore behind him, the actor could concentrate on his two next projects: the third series of ER and the biggest movie of his career to date, Batman and Robin.

Clooney was delighted to be reunited with award-winning ER director Mimi Leder during the making of The Peacemaker

Opposite: Clooney takes a time out for a drink during the filming of The Peacemaker

A box office disappointment, The Peacemaker still managed to win Clooney some great reviews for his dark and edgy performance

7

To the Batcave!

'The Batsuit is miserable ... But the deal is that you do that for five months and when it's done you get to be Batman'

On February 14th, 1996, the movie industry reeled at an unexpected announcement by Warner Bros. After just one film in the role, Val Kilmer would not be returning as the Caped Crusader in the fourth *Batman* blockbuster, *Batman and Robin*.

As *Batman and Robin*'s director, Joel Schumacher had the pick of virtually every actor in Hollywood to assume the prestigious (and lucrative) role of Bruce Wayne/Batman. He came up with the idea of casting George Clooney in the part during an airline flight. 'I opened the newspaper one day and saw an advert for *From Dusk Till Dawn* with his photo on,' Schumacher told *Film Review*. 'I took out a black marker pen, and for some reason drew the Bat cowl around him.

'I knew everyone was talking about *ER*, I don't have much time to watch television, so I watched the show and then saw *From Dusk Till Dawn* and got an idea of his range as an actor.'

Convinced that he had found the new Batman, Schumacher gave Clooney a phone call to ask if he would be interested in the role. The actor didn't have to think long about his reply.

'You're sitting at home and you get a call from Joel Schumacher,' he explained in *Empire*, 'and he says, "Hey, you wanna star in one of the biggest movies of all time and one of the greatest movie franchises in the world, and [a movie that] will give you a real shot at a film career?" You don't really pause. You just go, "Sure, when do we start filming?"'

Clooney and Schumacher sealed their deal after a meeting at Casa de Clooney, and the details were officially announced on February 26th. The leading role in *Batman and Robin* would earn the actor an amazing $10 million (five times the amount Kilmer was offered!) and was just the first part of a $28 million development deal Clooney had signed with Warner Bros. The studio also promised that Clooney's participation in *Batman and Robin* would not prevent him from appearing in the third season of its hit TV show, *ER*, and revealed that the actor had also agreed to work a seven-day week in order to fulfil both of his commitments.

Workload aside, Clooney wasn't too daunted by the prospect of stepping into the Batsuit. 'It's actually a lot less pressure being the third guy to play Batman,' he told *SFX* magazine. 'I think Val [Kilmer] had it tougher because Michael [Keaton] had done two ahead of him, but by the time I came along we'd kind of established that Batman was replaceable.'

Like all the *Batman* movies, *Batman and Robin* boasted a truly stellar cast. Besides George Clooney in the dual role of Bruce Wayne/Batman, the film featured action superstar Arnold Schwarzenegger (*Terminator*, *True Lies*) as the cold-hearted Mr Freeze, Uma Thurman (*Pulp Fiction*, *The Avengers*) as Poison Ivy, and *Clueless* sensation Alicia Silverstone as Barbara Wilson/Batgirl, while Chris O'Donnell reprised his role as Dick Grayson/Robin from the last instalment, *Batman Forever*. The movie's plotline follows the Dynamic Trio's battle to stop Mr Freeze and Poison Ivy from freezing Gotham City and turning it into a luscious jungle wilderness.

Right from the start, Joel Schumacher's prime goal for *Batman and Robin* was to infuse more humour into the franchise. Schumacher had scored a big hit with *Batman Forever* by abandoning many of the dark and adult overtones which had characterised Tim Burton's first two *Batman* movies, and hoped to find further success by continuing this trend in the fourth instalment.

As part of his plan, Schumacher ordered writer Akiva Goldsmith to 'lighten-up' the character of Bruce Wayne, and made it clear that Wayne should no longer feel tortured by his parents' murder. It was a decision that Clooney agreed with wholeheartedly.

'I think we've seen enough of the Bat-brooding,' the actor told *Cinescape*. 'I mean, let's think about it for a minute. Batman does not have such a tough life. The guy is

Despite his initial fears, Clooney really hit it off with co-star Arnold Schwarzenegger during the making of *Batman and Robin*

Opposite: **Cool as ice – Clooney's Batman leads Batgirl (Alicia Silverstone) and Robin (Chris O'Donnell) in the battle to save Gotham City**

loaded. He gets all the best girls. He has a cool car. What does Batman have to be depressed about?'

Despite its title, however, *Batman and Robin* was largely conceived as a showcase for Mr Freeze. To play the role, Arnold Schwarzenegger was paid $25 million and given a percentage of the film's profits from merchandising – which wasn't a bad deal, considering that he only spent six weeks on the production! The actor also received top-billing.

Whereas both Kilmer and Keaton had complained about the way that Batman was eclipsed by his deranged foes, Clooney was philosophical about the situation. 'The truth of the matter is that the star of this movie is not Batman,' he explained in *Batman and Robin: The Making of the Movie*. 'The criminals are always the star, because they're so much bigger than life. Batman is the constant, the steady in this. So my job is to be the foundation to hold all this together, because in a way the audience watches the movie through Batman's eyes.'

Batman and Robin began shooting in the second week of September, 1996. The movie was filmed Friday to Tuesday over five months, thus allowing Clooney a minimum of two days (Wednesday and Thursday) a week to work on *ER*. Although many actors would struggle to keep up with such a gruelling schedule, Joel Schumacher was impressed by Clooney's stamina and enthusiasm.

'He also goes out every night and he is having a full-blown romance,' the director noted in *Sci-Fi Universe*. 'I guess he should be playing Superman, not Batman.'

Clooney had little difficulty alternating between the roles of Dr Ross, Bruce Wayne and Batman.

'I don't have a whole lot of acting range anyway, so there isn't that much difference between the things I do,' the actor quipped in *SFX* magazine. 'I wish I could say I had a little more method to it, but I just show up, they stick me in the suit and I say, "Okay, what am I today?" As long as I don't have a stethoscope around the Batcave, I'm fine.' In fact, the only problem Clooney had on the set of *Batman and Robin* was wearing the Caped Crusader's rubber Batsuit. But even then, the actor refused to complain.

'The Batsuit is miserable,' he told *Film Review*. 'It's a nightmare. It's heavy, it's claustrophobic, but the deal is that you do that for five months and then when it's done you get to be Batman, so it's a trade-off.'

The batsuit soon became the target of one of Clooney's favourite jokes, as Schumacher revealed in *Cinescape*: 'He likes telling people he fit into Val's suit, but the codpiece had to be made much bigger!'

Aside from the trials and tribulations of squeezing into the Batsuit, Clooney's biggest worry about shooting *Batman and Robin* concerned the idea of working opposite Arnold Schwarzenegger. Fortunately, his initial fears proved completely ill-founded.

'I was worried about working with him,' he explained in *Satellite Times*. 'I'd met him quite

Men in black – Bruce Wayne (Clooney) and his loyal butler, Alfred Pennyworth (Michael Gough), consider Mr Freeze's latest scheme

a few times at Planet Hollywood and he's always been cool, really nice and funny, but I'd never worked with him. And you worry, especially if you're a guy, working opposite a giant male star. You just don't know. Things can change. But I walked into this situation and, man, he has been so nice, so fun to be around. He makes the set a blast. He's amazingly professional but also has a great time. I cannot say enough good things about him.'

The pair of actors obviously developed a rapport. During interviews, Schwarzenegger was full of praise for his co-star, while Clooney teased the action superstar ruthlessly. 'Arnold is really scared of me in real life,' he joked on Radio 1. 'We have a history, back when he was doing *Conan* … I stunt doubled for him!'

Despite the extensive demands of filming *Batman and Robin* and *ER* simultaneously, Clooney still managed to play his regular game of basketball every lunchtime. His team-mates included Chris O'Donnell, *ER*'s Eriq La Salle and Superman himself – alias Dean Cain, the star of the TV series *Lois & Clark: The New Adventures of Superman*. Clooney was adamant that the Dynamic Duo always beat the Man of Steel on the court!

Unfortunately, while Superman is virtually indestructible, Batman is not – as Clooney found out just before the end of shooting *Batman and Robin*, when he sprained his ankle during a basketball game

'I was trying to prove that white men can jump,' he later joked. 'They just don't know how to land!' As a result of the injury, Clooney

A dynamic duo on and off the set – Clooney and co-star Chris O'Donnell made an unbeatable team on the basketball court!

spent the rest of his time on the film hobbling on his crutches.

Apart from that slight mishap, the production of *Batman and Robin* went like a dream. Principal photography concluded in the third week of January, no less than two weeks ahead of schedule, and the film came in at slightly less than its expected $90 million budget.

The production went so smoothly, in fact, that Schumacher was approached by Warner chiefs Bob Daly and Terry Semel shortly before the end of shooting, and asked if he would consider directing the fifth *Batman* movie. It was an offer Schumacher felt morally obliged to accept.

'I asked George and Chris to play these roles, and if *Batman and Robin* is successful and another Batman movie were to be planned, I would not then say to them, "Well, gee, thanks a lot for helping me out guys, but you're on your own, go find someone else. Bye." I think it would be unethical. Also,' the director added, 'it's just too much fun. I would be jealous if someone else got this.'

Clooney expressed a similar interest in returning to the franchise. He revealed that his contract contained an option for two further *Batman* films, and claimed he had already come up with some ideas for the next film. 'I think we should kill off Robin and Batgirl in the next one,' he said with his tongue firmly in his cheek.

The actor's work and his behaviour on set won the respect of everyone around him. Joel Schumacher was one of his chief admirers. 'Besides being a wonderful actor,' the director told *SFX*, 'and looking mighty handsome in that black rubber, he's brought a humanity to the role.'

Impressed by Clooney's performance, Warner chiefs asked the actor if he would be interested in taking the lead role in *Frosty*, a feature film adaptation of the classic song *Frosty the Snowman*! The brainchild of cult director Sam Raimi (*The Evil Dead*, *Darkman*), the family-orientated movie would star Clooney as a jazz musician who dies in a car accident, but returns to Earth as a (computer-generated) snowman to look after the child he neglected before his death. Clooney agreed, but left the project when it became trapped in development hell, and was replaced by original *Batman* star Michael Keaton.

Clooney was philosophical about the Caped Crusader being eclipsed by Mr Freeze in *Batman and Robin*. 'The criminals are always the star,' he explained

With *Batman and Robin* in the can, Clooney returned to the Emergency Room full-time. And he continued to thoroughly enjoy working on the show as it entered its third year.

'I'm really excited about some of the storylines that are going on,' he explained in *Film Review*. 'I think the AIDS storyline that we're doing with Gloria Reuben [Jeanie Boulet in the series] is so strong. I think it's really great because we've seen people before on television that are HIV-positive, but now we are going to watch her continue to live and function well on the show, and I think that's really important because that's what people are doing.'

The series hit the headlines shortly after its third season premiere, when Warner announced that Sherry Stringfield would be leaving the show. The popular actress, who played Dr Lewis, had grown tired of the daily rigours of series television and wanted to pursue her stage career in New York. Although many reporters wondered if *ER* could survive her departure, Clooney made it clear that the show would go on. 'The star of the show is the show,' he said. 'I love and adore Sherry. She is very talented, but the show won't even skip a beat.' As Clooney's *ER* salary rocketed up to $100,000 per episode at the start of its third season, it was clear than Warner chiefs were determined to get their money's worth. Consequently, on top of the usual medical emergencies, the season saw Doug's long-brewing relationship with Nurse Hathaway step up a gear, and also had the delectable doctor befriending a teenage prostitute, Charlene 'Charlie' Chiemienga (played by *Interview with the Vampire*'s Kirsten Dunst).

By the end of *ER*'s third season, it was clear that Clooney's confidence in the show was not ill-founded. It remained America's most-watched TV show, generating audiences of around 32 million [viewers] each week, and was once again critically-applauded, collecting a People's Choice Award, a Screen Actors' Guild Award and a further Emmy nomination for 'Best Series'. For his efforts, Clooney was voted 'Sexiest Man Alive' by *People* magazine and was also named 'Best Dressed Male Television Star.'

As *ER* weathered a potential storm, *Batman and Robin* was heading for the rocks. The first warning sign that the film was not going to be the blockbuster everyone expected it to be came in April 1997, when *Batman and Robin* was test-screened for a sample audience. The audience simply hated the film and actually began booing during certain scenes!

The test-screening proved to be an accurate reflection of the world's response to the film. Critics and die-hard Bat-fans alike hated it. The movie's (razor-thin) plot was a carbon clone of *Batman Forever*, while Schumacher's emphasis on humour had cost the movie any dramatic resonance. To make matters worse, the director completely wasted his all-star cast; Clooney, in particular, was given little of interest to do.

Reviews of *Batman and Robin* were universally bad: comments like 'Caped crusader strikes out!' (*The Chicago Tribune*), 'It's loud, long, pointless' (*The Philadelphia Inquirer*) and 'Over-choreographed, over-crowded, over thetop chaos' (*The Detroit Free Press*) were the norm. In America, *Batman and Robin* took a disappointing $107.3 million – less than *Men in Black*, *The Lost World: Jurassic Park 2* and even the re-release of *Star Wars*! This provided a stark contrast to *Batman Forever*, which had been the top-grossing film of 1995. Following the film's launch, a number of rumours concerning the franchise's future began to circulate. Most reports claimed that Schumacher would not be involved in any further *Batman* movies. A small number suggested that another actor would don the Batsuit next time out, and Clint Eastwood was said to be favourite to replace Clooney as the Caped Crusader! Towards the end of 1997, Clooney himself commented on the film's disappointing performance. Refusing to blame Schumacher or any one individual for the movie's failure, he promised that *Batman 5* would be better.

'When I saw the movie I was disappointed,' he admitted in *Film Review*. 'I know it didn't work on a lot of different levels, so you can't point fingers at anybody or any particular thing.'

The response to the the film threatened to destroy the Bat franchise and also cast a dark cloud over George Clooney's movie career.

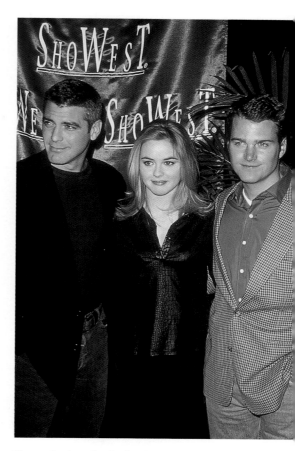

Clooney's plans for the inevitable *Batman 5*? 'I think we should kill off Robin and Batgirl,' he frequently joked

Out of Sight

8

Whatever the future holds, you can be sure that George Clooney will try to enjoy life to the full. And he's determined to make the most out of his career for as long as it lasts

The fourth season of *ER* opened with the most ambitious episode in the show's history: an episode which was performed and broadcast live across America on September 25th, 1997. George Clooney couldn't complain about the series' risky experiment, as it originally was his idea to go live with *ER*.

'About halfway through the first season of the show,' Clooney told *Film Review*, 'when we got better at doing these long one-shot trauma scenes, I said to the gang, "We've got to do this live." I talked with [executive producer] John Wells and he thought I was on drugs! I got Tony Edwards involved and we went to the studio and then we went to the network. We kept saying, "Guys this would do well. We can probably get a 50 share out of this."' They agreed.

'John Wells came to us at the end of the [third] season and said, "Okay, you wanted to do it live, you got it. Don't come whining to me!"'

Entitled *Ambush*, the fourth season premiere followed a day in Cook County Hospital through the eyes of a visiting documentary crew. To raise the stakes for *ER* cast and crew, the episode actually had to be performed twice, so that it could be broadcast live to both America's East and West coasts.

Just prior to the show's transmission, Clooney admitted to feeling a little stage fright. 'People will watch us like they're watching the Indy 500 [car race],' he explained. 'They don't go to see you go around in a circle 300 times, they want to see you crash and burn!'

For whatever reason, *Ambush* was certainly a success in the ratings. Watched by an audience of 60 million viewers, it was the highest-rated season premiere in the history of American TV, and the country's fourth most-watched TV programme of all time. And if Clooney's prediction that people were tuning in to spot mistakes was true, most viewers would have been disappointed; the cast and crew went through their paces with ease, and the only errors were the occasional mispronunciation of medical jargon.

Following its high-profile début, *ER*'s fourth season enjoyed an 11 per cent increase in its ratings from the previous season, making it the most successful fourth-year drama series since *Dallas*. These figures were no doubt boosted by Dr Ross' ongoing romance with Nurse Hathaway. After three years, the pair finally became an item. Viewers were delighted when Doug finally asked Carol to marry him – and were then completely shocked by her reply.

ER's rising ratings were probably a key factor in NBC's decision to commission a sixth and seventh season of the show. In January 1998, details emerged that the network had agreed to pay $13 million per episode (a $5 million increase) to keep the show on air until the spring of 2001.

However, the announcement of ER's continuation into the 21st Century was somewhat eclipsed by the revelation that Clooney had declined an offer to extend his contract beyond the original five-year deal. Although the rest of his cast-mates had agreed to stay with the show, Clooney seemed set to leave the Emergency Room in 1999.

Opposite: **Despite persistent rumours to the contrary, Clooney is adamant that he won't be marrying his girlfriend, Céline Balitan**

Clooney's decision wasn't surprising at all. He had always said that he would fulfil his five-year contract with *ER*, but never expressed any interest in remaining aboard indefinitely. He also had a flourishing film career to consider. Nevertheless, the media proceeded to make a major story out of his decision, and reports soon began to appear claiming that the producers were planning to kill Dr Ross off at the end of the show's fourth year!

'His character will be shot in the ER and killed in an awful and bloody rampage by a gang member,' an unnamed scriptwriter reportedly told *Now* magazine. 'It won't be pretty, but life in *ER* often isn't, which is what the show has always been about.'

As the story became more elaborate, the 'reasons' for Clooney's sudden change of heart emerged. Apparently, Céline was unhappy with his extremely busy work schedule, and felt that he was not devoting as much time to their romance as he might have.

Fortunately, the truth behind Clooney's

future with *ER* soon began to re-emerge. The actor's spokesman announced that he still intended to fulfil his original contract and hoped to stay aboard until the spring of 1999. And John Wells confirmed that Clooney would almost certainly be a part of the show's fifth season.

'He's been fairly clear in saying that he plans to honour his original commitment,' the producer explained in *Now*, 'but that afterwards he wants to pursue his feature-film career. I'll be sorry to see him go.'

Wells won't be the only one. Millions of viewers around the world will be devastated by Doug Ross' departure from the Emergency Room. Clooney himself has admitted that he will miss playing the good doctor. Consequently, it's unlikely that the character will be killed off; the door will probably be left open for him to return to the show, either on an occasional basis or as a series regular, should he reconsider his decision or find his film career faltering.

Not that there's much chance of that happening, though. Despite the disappointing performance of *Batman and Robin*, Clooney is still one of filmdom's hottest commodities and his schedule is simply jam-packed with movies. One of the most eagerly-awaited is *Out of Sight*, a romantic thriller based on the best-selling Elmore Leonard novel and directed by Steven Soderbergh (*Sex, Lies and Videotape*). The film stars Clooney as Jack Foley, a charming bank robber who escapes from prison and takes a female Federal Marshal, Karen Cisco (*Anaconda*'s Jennifer Lopez) hostage – only to fall in love with her. Shot on location across midwest America, *Out of Sight* promises to showcase Clooney's strengths as both an action hero and romantic lead.

Following *Out of Sight*, Clooney is next up in *The Thin Red Line*. The first film to be directed by Terrence Malick since *Days of Heaven* in 1978, *The Thin Red Line* is a remake of the 1964 wartime drama which chronicles the experiences of three army officers in the Battle of Guadalcanal in 1942. The film features a trio of relatively unknown actors in the lead roles, namely Adrien Brody, Jim Caviezel and Ben Chaplin, but boasts a remarkable supporting cast which includes not only Clooney but also John Cusack,

ER's fourth season kicked off in style, with an episode performed and broadcast live across America in September 1997

Woody Harrelson, Nick Nolte, Sean Penn, Bill Pullman, John Savage and John Travolta. The film is expected to win kudos for Clooney, and is tipped for numerous awards.

As a result of his commitments to *ER* and *The Thin Red Line*, Clooney reluctantly had to abandon his plans to star in *The Wild, Wild West*, the feature film adaptation of the popular 1960s' TV series. Directed by Barry Sonnenfeld (*Men in Black*, *Get Shorty*), the movie was set to star Clooney alongside Will Smith (*Independence Day*, *Men in Black*), until Clooney realised that he would not be able to meet the film's proposed April 1998 start date.

Beyond *The Thin Red Line*, Clooney has a host of film projects in development with Warner Brothers, including the comedies *Metal God*, *Zig Zag* and *How To Start Your Own Country*, the political thriller *Heat Score*, the prison drama *Move!*, the romantic comedy *A Thousand Kisses* and the Civil War drama *His Promised Land*. The actor will either topline or produce these projects once they begin filming, and his first production credit will be on the thriller *Five Past Midnight*.

In the longer term, Clooney may yet star in *The Green Hornet*, the film project he abandoned in 1996 to make *The Peacemaker*. However, he might wish to restrict his comic-strip heroics to the inevitable fifth *Batman* film. Warner chiefs are bound to revive the flagging franchise at some point in the future, and the latest rumours suggest that the fifth instalment will pit Clooney against two more of the Dark Knight's comic-strip villains, The Scarecrow and Harley Quinn.

Just as he spent much of his career as a TV star without a hit TV show to his name, George Clooney remains a film star who has yet to have a resounding, truly blockbusting hit at the box office. Fortunately, it's a situation the actor can live with. 'I've had moderate success with all the projects I've had come out,' he noted in *Empire*, 'and not huge, great success with any of them. That's okay.'

While Clooney hopes that major movie success is ahead of him, he has no complaints about the way his career has developed since he stepped on the set of *And They're Off*, way back in 1981. 'I'm more successful than I ever thought I would be,' he said. 'I've been lucky enough to be on one television series or another for the last 15 years, and if you're

an actor in this business and you're making a living at all, then you're one of only a few that is.'

Clooney knows that he won't be Hollywood's hottest property forever, though. Having learned all about the fickle nature of success in showbusiness as a child growing up in the 1960s, he is ready for the inevitable fall from grace. As part of his game plan, he has begun to move into other mediums, namely writing and producing. Besides his aforementioned film projects, Clooney has developed a TV series for the NBC network. Thus, as he pointed out in the *Radio Times*: 'When everyone is sick of me as I am, I'll have these other places to go to work and make an income.'

Should Clooney ever feel like leaving showbusiness altogether, he might be wise to try a career in politics. While the actor has laughed off such suggestions in the past, he has a strong interest in current affairs and clearly takes his responsibilities as a public figure very seriously. For instance, following the tragic death of Diana, Princess of Wales in 1997, Clooney advocated a privacy law and launched a vehement attack on the paparazzi: 'I wonder how you people sleep at night,' he stated. 'You should be ashamed.'

Of course, one of the biggest question marks hanging over Clooney concerns his

Still a critical and commercial sensation, *ER* looks set to continue well into the 21st century – with or without George Clooney

Always wanting to 'live life to the full', Clooney isn't content to just relax by the beach during his vacation!

status as Hollywood's most confirmed bachelor. The tabloids have frequently speculated that he will find himself married with kids one day; indeed, both Michelle Pfeiffer and Nicole Kidman have money riding on him becoming a father! Clooney, however, is adamant that it won't happen.

'No way I am going to lose my money on this one,' he claimed in *The Express*. 'The deal is for 20 grand. I can get a vasectomy for $5,000 and I'm $15,000 up. Right there I can make a profit!'

Whatever the future holds, you can be sure that George Clooney will try to enjoy life to the full. And he is determined to make the most out of his career for as long as it lasts.

'I'm really enjoying the ride for what it's worth,' he told *Movie Idols* magazine. 'And I'm very grateful.'

Although George Clooney has always predicted that his spectacular career would grind to a halt one day, he may yet have to eat his words. As time goes by, he has an increasingly good shot at becoming a perennial movie star, alongside the likes of Tom Cruise, Harrison Ford and Mel Gibson. So hold on tight, George – the ride may have only just begun.

Opposite: Despite his extensive film and TV commitments, Clooney remains a keen basketball player. And he doesn't like to lose!

Below: Although he's ready for the day when his career grinds to a halt, George Clooney looks set to remain one of Hollywood's hottest properties for many years to come

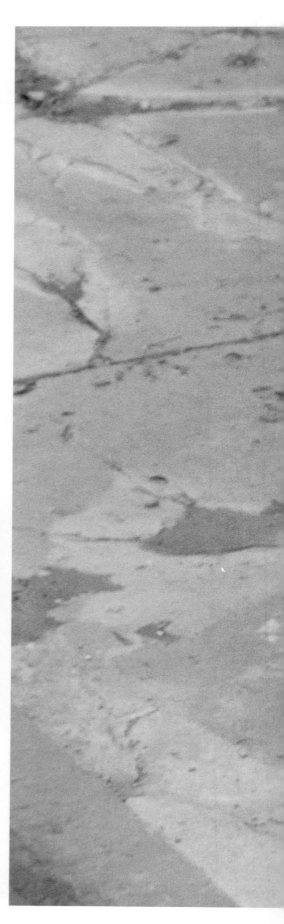

Selected Credits

FILMS

1982 *And They're Off*

1983 *Grizzly II – The Predator*

1986 *Combat High (also known as Combat Academy)*

1987 *Return to Horror High (TV movie)*

1988 *Return of the Killer Tomatoes!*

1990 *Red Surf*

1992 *Unbecoming Age (also known as The Magic Bubble)*

1993 *The Harvest*

1993 *Without Warning: Terror in the Towers (TV movie)*

1995 *From Dusk Till Dawn*

1996 *One Fine Day*

1997 *Batman and Robin*

1997 *The Peacemaker*

1998 *Out of Sight*

1998 *The Thin Red Line*

TELEVISION

1984 *E/R*

1985 *The Facts of Life*

1988 *Roseanne*

1990 *Sunset Beat*

1990 *Baby Talk*

1991 *Knights of the Kitchen*

1992 *Bodies of Evidence*

1993 *Sisters*

1994 *ER*

TV GUEST-STARRING ROLES

1985 *The Golden Girls*

1987 *Hunter*

1987 *Murder, She Wrote*

1993 *The Building*

1995 *Friends*

1997 *South Park (voice only)*